SAMSON AGONISTES

SAMSON AGONISTES
a re-dramatisation after Milton

JOHN KINSELLA

with an Introduction by
Stephen Chinna
and an Afterword by
Tim Cribb

Published by Arc Publications,
Nanholme Mill, Shaw Wood Road
Todmorden OL14 6DA, UK
www.arcpublications.co.uk

Copyright in the poetic text © John Kinsella, 2018
Copyright in the Introduction © Stephen Chinna, 2018
Copyright in the Afterword © Tim Cribb, 2018
Copyright in the present edition © Arc Publications, 2018

978 1911469 55 1 (pbk)
978 1911469 56 8 (ebk)

Design by Tony Ward
Cover design by Tony Ward

Cover picture:
Roman mosaic unearthed in a fifth-cenury Israeli synagogue in the ancient village of Huqoq in Israel's lower Galilee.

Acknowledgements

The author wishes to thank the editor of *Island* magazine for material printed in issue 156; Stephen Chinna and Tim Cribb for their respective Introduction and Afterword to this volume; the Marlowe Society and the Judith E. Wilson Studio, Cambridge University for the premier studio performance of the author's dramatisation on 24 October 2018, directed by Ruby Morris; Churchill College, Cambridge and Curtin University, Western Australia; and finally James Byrne, Tony Ward and Angela Jarman at Arc Publications.

This book is in copyright. Subject to statutory exception and to provision of relevant collective licensing agreements, no reproduction of any part of this book may take place without the written permission of Arc Publications.

**International Editor:
James Byrne**

*For Israel and Palestine and lasting peace,
justice and equality in all things*

CONTENTS

Stephen Chinna –
'The Shifting Paradox: Bondage or 'Strenuous Liberty'?
An Introduction / 9

John Kinsella
Samson Agonistes:
An intertextual re-dramatisation after Milton / 25

Tim Cribb – 'Fit and Few'
An Afterword / 88

Biographical Notes / 108

The Shifting Paradox: Bondage or 'Strenuous Liberty'?
Stephen Chinna

PREAMBLE

Samson. Is it ever just Samson, or is it invariably a couple? Samson and Delilah: what resonances does that pairing of names throw up? Samson. Son of Sam. Surely not David Berkowitz? Delilah. 'I saw the light on the night...'. So many song references, either in the title of an old blues song, 'Samson and Delilah', recorded in 1977 by the Grateful Dead, or in the verses of various songs. It would appear that Samson and Delilah are popular culture namedrops. What do I know of this story? I was brought up Anglican, so Sunday School stories informed me of this narrative of carnage, betrayal, and revenge, and the perfidy of women. But as a child I heard, and later read, an Aussie joke – the story of 'Simpson and Delicious' and how the 'Filipinos' were slain with 'the arsebone' of what shall remain unnamed, but it was certainly no 'trivial weapon' as Milton's Chorus term it. At some time in the same period I also experienced Victor Mature and Hedy Lamarr in Cecil B. DeMille's 1949 *Samson and Delilah* at the Margaret River town hall pictures – a once a week film event on a rolling circuit of south-western towns in Western Australia, run by an ex-timberworker, Alan Jones, whose voiceover on the previews would talk of the 'fillums' to come. As well as films from the 1920s to the present which take the eponymous couple as their subjects, there is also Warwick Thornton's 2009 Australian film, *Samson and Delilah*, an almost voiceless narrative, and in Thornton's words a 'survival love story', portraying two Australian Aboriginal teenagers combating a life of ennui and desperation in the country around Alice Springs. And then there was, and still is, an image in my King James Bible, presented to me on my leaving of the Far Cotton Sunday School in Northampton, England before departing for Australia. I was six and would have preferred a train set. It was an OUP publication, the full adult version, but contained several colour plates, perhaps for children, perhaps for colonials. An uncredited painting entitled 'Samson and The Philistines' shows a bare-chested Samson being overpowered and tied up by a bunch of swarthy piratical looking Philistines, while in the background the perfidious Delilah glances fearfully back as she flees the scene.

The tale of Samson, and hence Delilah, has had many tellings, and variations on the narrative exist across cultures and times, especially in epic tales of a hero of superhuman strength who is brought down by his own hubris, and invariably through the wiles of a woman hired by the hero's enemies to undo him thorough some form of seduction and sophistry. Whether it be Hercules or a modern superhero, the archetype doesn't alter too much. But what we are concerned with here are two poetic / dramatic treatments of the tale, one, *Samson Agonistes* by the seventeenth-century English poet John Milton, and the other, *Samson Agonistes: An intertextual re-dramatisation after Milton*, by the twenty-first century Australian poet, John Kinsella.

Two Samsons

To start with John Milton. Milton's 'dramatic poem' *Samson Agonistes* was first published in 1671, along with his *Paradise Regained*. Why does Milton take this particular story from the Old Testament *Book of Judges* as a follow-up to his *Paradise Lost* and *Paradise Regained*? What purpose does Milton's text serve? It was not Milton's first published engagement with the story – among others, in Book IX of *Paradise Lost* he writes:

> *So rose the Danite strong*
> *Hercúlean Samson from the harlot-lap*
> *Of Philistéan Dálilah, and waked*
> *Shorn of his strength...* (IX, lines 1059-1062)[1]

[1] See Hone, p. 94, for this and other references to Samson by Milton.

Milton doesn't just write this 'dramatic poem' because he's in the mood for giving the Samson and Delilah story a poetic treatment in the style of 'Aeschylus, Sophocles, and Euripides, the three tragic poets unequalled yet by any' as he mentions in his introduction, 'Of that Sort of Dramatic Poem called Tragedy'.[2] Milton certainly has an agenda, but he doesn't set it out in his Argument. Rather, Milton proffers a synopsis of the narrative, and nothing more. But what is Milton's agenda here? Is Milton the 'propagandist' as Kinsella's Harapha terms him (p. 66)? Well, yes, of course he is a propagandist. Then what is his 'message'? Mary Ann Radzinowicz, in her chapter "The Political Significance of *Samson Agonistes*' tells us that Milton wrote this as an 'exemplary tragedy for his nation', and as an educative drama for the English public. Like many of his political poems it was composed with 'an agonistic pattern moving through catharsis to harmony'.[3] One can go on to research the historical context but it is enough to know here that Milton was a fervent supporter of the Puritan Revolution which led to the English Civil War, and that he bemoaned the retreat back to Absolutism with the Restoration. Milton was an unapologetic supporter for the removal and execution of Charles I and an avid publicist for Oliver Cromwell, so it is no wonder he went into hiding when Charles II and his retinue reappeared into English politics and onto the London court scene.

For Milton, Samson's tale concerns a blinded hero who, notwithstanding his past faults, leads by the example of his self-sacrifice to educate his people of the dangers of their self-bondage to a system that limits, or even prohibits individual free will. This is a central point of Milton's poem, tied into his beliefs in free will tempered with an understanding of contingent predestination. This is a complex argument concerning Puritan predestination

---

[2] Hone, p. 5.
[3] Radzinowicz, p. 167.

versus that of contingent predestination, or what was known as the Arminian heresy, and this is not the place to furnish more detail other than pointing out with the latter that the individual can thus have some agency in finding grace, rather than it being purely bestowed by God.[4] In short, Milton saw Samson as a necessarily flawed hero who must therefore struggle to be redeemed and be the saviour of his people. It is important to know that Milton was completely blind by 1652 and dictated his poems to his daughters and various other assistants, and thus the quality of sound is crucial to an understanding of Milton's works, and no less of John Kinsella's poetry. Poetry is written to be spoken, and heard. For Milton, *Samson Agonistes* was a poem to be listened to, not for 'the stage (to which this work never was intended)'.[5] And here we have John Kinsella's poetic and intertextual reworking of John Milton's dramatic poem. Does Kinsella echo Milton's themes, or some of them? Does he compose this out of an admiration for Milton's poetics, for his strength, for his courage? Along with many others, Milton has long been part of Kinsella's poetic influences. For example, there is his treatment of Milton's 1634 masque *Comus*, reworked as *Comus: A Dialogic Mask*, staged by the Marlowe Society at Christ's College, Cambridge in June 2008, and published by Arc Publications in the same year. Another is his *Paradise Lust. A Poem. Book I: Damage Report*, published in 2012.

Rather than offering only a synopsis, in his 'Argument' Kinsella asks which 'version of a story are we being privileged to hear?'. And, 'what are the agendas?'. He states: 'This is a tale of conflicted belief, values, and desires' and both certainly are narratives of 'conflicted belief, values, and desires'. And they both deliberately embrace situations where 'paradoxes multiply'. Does Kinsella echo Milton's themes, or some of them? Yes. In a similar fashion

---

[4] See more on this on Radzinowicz, pp. 339-47.
[5] John Milton. '*Samson Agonistes*: A Dramatic Poem'. In Hone, p. 5.

to Milton, his 'pacifist text' has a focus on how Samson, a paradoxical symbol of uncontrolled violence, as well as being a pacifist peacemaker and the possessor of a cyborg sensitivity, must come to terms with his participation in his own powerlessness and incarceration.

Samson, a Judge, a Demi-angel, and a Cyborg

Samson is no ordinary mortal. In the Bible he is a major judge, a leader, one of twelve who 'judged Israel' for twenty years (*Judges* XV 20). In a similar fashion to the Samson of the Bible and Milton, a hybrid creation miraculously conceived in a meeting between a 'barren' woman and an angel, Kinsella's Samson is also a hybrid, here part human, part cyborg. Not unlike many heroes of the Old Testament, Samson, whether the demi-angel Samson of Milton or the cyborg Samson of Kinsella, is yet another 'fierce destroyer' as Milton's Dalila labels him (line 985), and in Kinsella's reworking, a

> weaponised self, this cyborg proto-
> type that is me guided by angels, drone
> operators who go home to above
> average income lifestyle church and state
> lifestyles. (p. 29)

A cyborg Samson makes sense – it certainly makes more sense in a secular and digital age than a Samson who is the issue of a conception of the 'barren' wife of Manoah as described in *Judges* XIII 2. This 'very terrible' angel of the Lord that materialises in the cornfields, sweet-talking the wives of absent men, obviously echoes other angelic messengers delivering news of immaculate conceptions. It raises the question of how much agency is allowed any of these figures. Both Samsons are largely determined by the powers that rule over them, whether the Old Testament God or digital software. Both are 'designed for mass destruction, / for such a fait accompli destiny' (p. 30). Kinsella's Samson recognises that he is a tool, a convenient humanoid weapon system fused with technology with echoes of a Schwarzeneggerian destruction machine. In his opening address, that smoothly segues from Milton into Kinsella, this blind Samson in chains can reflect as the 'sea people' celebrate their sun worship:

> But I am the fool
> to be so readily deployed and used
> by their offices. The self's paradox:
> *in power of others, never in my own;*
> *scarce half I seem to live, dead more than half.*
> *o dark, dark, dark, amid the blaze of noon,*　　　　80
> *irrecoverably dark, total Eclipse*
> *without all hope of day!* (p. 31)

This is the first incursion, infection, invasion, or perhaps rather invitation, of the 'old grey poet' Milton's words into Kinsella's text, and they don't jar. The texts reverberate against one another – sometimes almost merging, at other times clashing, not so much in their rhythms as in their contextual sensibilities. Furthermore, there is that first paradox invoked, that 'self's paradox' where the whole is not composed of two equal halves, but an unequal division between life and death, light and darkness, day and night. Both Samsons exist in this paradoxical state between polarities, always already the 'paradox in which other paradoxes multiply'.

Kinsella's paradoxical Samson is both killer and peacemaker, both similar and different to Milton's problematic protagonist who, like his Biblical forerunner, partakes of a libertine life of consorting with other tribes, 'bonding' with foreigners, and engaging in the deliberate slaughter of hundreds, or even thousands of his enemies, even those within his own tribal group. But now we have a Samson reworked, who, so the Chorus maintain, 'paused the slaughter / by standing between all warring / peoples' (p. 33). This is very different behaviour to Milton's Samson, who with

> *The jaw of a dead ass, his sword of bone,*
> *A thousand foreskins fell, the flower of Palestine,*
> *In Ramath-lechi, famous to this day:* (lines 143-45)

There is a skilful merging with Milton in what follows in this second major engagement with the source text, where Milton's construction of Samson as the weaponless killing machine is subverted by presenting him

> as individual, as *person* –
> ran on embattelld Armies clad in Iron,
> and weaponless himself,
> made Arms ridiculous, useless the forgery
> of brazen shield and spear, the hammer'd Cuirass,
> Chalybean temper'd steel, and frock of mail
> Adamantean Proof;
> but safest he who stood aloof –
> who refused warcraft, who refused
> to value one life over another! (p. 33)

Kinsella here reworks Milton's retelling of the Biblical story of Samson's courage and power drawn into the service of Milton's anti-Restoration agenda to create a Samson who is a peacemaker, a pacifist – seeking 'not to oppress oppressors but disarm and make them ineffective' (p. 36).

But for Samson's father, Manoah, this is a 'miserable change!' (p. 40). Samson's 'angel skills' have been put to sounder use in complying to his tribe's 'lethal ways' (p. 40), even though he is now blind and powerless, and no longer 'slaughtering' their enemies. And Manoah recognises the paradox – that their enemies are the same as he and his people, caught up in a warring culture that in some ways blindly seeks a mutually assured destruction.

> Sure, we'd do the same if the shoe was on
> The other foot, but it's no time for jokes. (p. 43)

There is an ambiguity here concerning Samson and his 'lethal ways'. The difficulty is in disentangling this contemporary Samson from those of the Old Testament story and of Milton's dramatic poem. Both poets write their Samsons within worlds of intertribal, civil, and national warfare. Samson's Biblical slaughters, even given the context in relation to relative population numbers and the seemingly hyperbolically inflated figures, obviously pale in comparison to the mass slaughters of the twentieth century. The contemporary world has no shortage of savage conflicts, but Kinsella's Samson claims that he 'didn't kill anyone' (p. 43). Could this be read as a paradoxical denial, or moral evasion, of his own participation in slaughter, a shelving of responsibility for his actions onto his software-generated deterministic programming – a variation on 'The Devil made me do it'? But it appears that this contemporary Samson is a not a war machine:

> I have sought not to oppress oppressors
> but disarm and make them ineffective. (p. 36)

However, the exchanges between Samson and Manoah, who bemoans the fact that their 'rivals' are celebrating because Samson is 'no longer slaughtering them', builds on the ambiguities and paradoxes of this Samson, who while serving as a signifier for an early-twenty-first century eco-consciousness, also carries the residues of his Judaic and literary forebears, as well as the programming over which he has no control. To return to the point made earlier concerning the Arminian heresy and the concept of a contingent predestination, Milton's Samson struggles to exercise the free will which his God has granted him and like Milton's Samson, Kinsella's Samson also must struggle against the programming of his god – in this case, Artificial Intelligence:

> When my mother and my father
> are not allowed responsibility,
> I – preordained, predestined, constructed –
> roll off the AI production line. I –
> evil and good and trending and hashtagged.
> I – no petition can save me
> from what they – you all! — have manufactured. (p. 49)

As Manoah comes to see, Samson is no longer a killer, the 'old ways are not his ways now' (p. 79) and in the final scenes, offstage in the temple, he sacrifices the human part of him, dying a necessary death, as does Milton's Samson. There is so much more that could be said about these Samsons, and some will be, but what of Dalila? In the procession of characters that move through the narrative, Manoah's exit to plead his son's case is followed by Dalila's entrance.

DALILA – MY WIFE! MY TRAITRESS!

The Biblical Delilah, or Dalila (as she will be hereafter referred), has invariably been seen as a symbol of treachery, reflecting a fear of women across many societies and cultures. Sometimes they are worshipped, sometimes they are damned, and the Dalilas of these treatments of *Samson Agonistes* reflect their writers' times and beliefs. On her arrival, Milton's Dalila is likened to a vessel on the water – a mystery that comes into view:

> *But who is this? what thing of sea or land –*
> *Female of sex it seems –*
> *That so bedecked, ornate, and gay,*
> *Comes this way sailing,*
> *Like a stately ship* (lines 710-14).

This is no woman of flesh and blood; as well as being a 'thing', this is an image of power and grace. But while she may appear like a 'some rich Philistian matron' (line 722), she is also a 'traitress' (line 725), and a 'hyaena' (line 748), and a 'sorceress' (line 819) – among other epithets. But Dalila, necessarily, admits her faults, and confesses that her 'weakness' is 'incident to all our sex' and really, after all, it is Samson's fault for the ills that have befallen him for having 'trusted' to a woman's 'frailty' (lines 773-83).

Milton's Dalila is ambiguously characterised, as both deceitful weak woman and powerful recogniser of the hypocrisy of the Biblical casting of her as villainess and traitress. She is constructed as the wicked wayward woman – a seductress and betrayer, who like Judas, sells out a hero for pieces of silver. The Bible says Samson loves Dalila, or at least Dalila says he does, but it doesn't say she loves him. And she 'presses' him until he tells her the secret of his great strength. Dalila then disappears from the Biblical account, and when Samson dies in the temple, along with about three thousand men and women, there is no mention of Dalila being present to meet her end. According to the Biblical story, she does betray him for money, but, after all, he is an enemy of her people. Shouldn't that make her a champion of her people? In Bob Dylan's 'Tombstone Blues' (1965), he makes several references to the Samson story but the telling lines concern 'Delilah, who's sitting worthlessly alone / But the tears on her cheeks are from laughter'.[6] This 'Delilah' is unrepentant and my thoughts went to another Old Testament woman who seduces a man in order to betray him – Judith, who severs the head of the Assyrian general Holofernes from his body. As Howard Barker's Judith says after doing the deed: 'I think I could cut off a million heads and go home amiable as if I had been scything in the meadow.'[7] However, Judith's story does not make it into the Old Testament and remains a part of the Apocrypha. So why is Dalila the perfidious betrayer of a hero, and Judith not? Well, obviously it depends whose side you are on – Judith is an Israelite, Holofernes an Assyrian, and Dalila is, presumably, a Philistine. In Milton's treatment, Dalila recognises this double standard, stating, *'Fame, if not double-faced, is double-mouthed' / And with contrary blast proclaims most deeds;'* (lines 971-2). She invokes the story of Jael, the Israelite widow, who nails the Canaanite commander Sisera's head to the ground with a tent peg, and informs Samson that she, Dalila, will be counted among

> *the famousest*
> *Of women, sung at solemn festivals,*
> *Living and dead recorded, who, to save*
> *Her country from a fierce destroyer, chose*
> *Above the faith of wedlock bands;* (lines 982-86).

---

[6] 1965. M. Witmark & Sons, USA.
[7] Howard Barker 'Judith. A Parting from the Body.' *Howard Barker. Collected Plays 3*. London: Calder, 1996, p. 264.

Milton's withholding of judgement on Dalila echoes his treatment of Eve in his *Paradise Lost* (although his Chorus may suggest otherwise) and that of Kinsella places her firmly within a conception informed by a recognition and acceptance of contemporary feminist politics and sensibilities. Kinsella's Dalila recognises the entrapment that both she and Samson share in their 'trials and tribulations' of 'patriarchal bullshit' (p. 54). There is an acknowledgement of a joint, or even conjoined, blindness to how their own self-hate or blind faith in custom and bondage to religious and cultural division steers their destinies. But Dalila sees past this blindness, as does Samson in his more lucid moments when not driven by the programming of his artificial intelligence. As she says, it 'Takes two to tango, partner, and we have to own our assured mutual destruction' (p. 52). The exchange between Dalila and Samson highlights the paradoxes and contradictions of their faiths, allegiances and senses of betrayal. Who is right here? Dalila seems to recognise, like Samson, how they are caught within their own narrative, the systems of power and control always already manipulated by others. All Dalila wants is Samson to also acknowledge his complicity in these systems of control, and to 'speak out' for those who are oppressed by patriarchal strictures of misogyny, racism, and cultural repression. But then there is another figure who approaches, the giant Harapha, who recognises and tacitly speaks of an oppression, that repressive determinism which corrals him into a programmed behaviour.

Harapha signifies a trust in military technology. It is a rigidity that entraps him as part of a war machine, echoing so much of the rhetoric of military training, of masculine bravado and comradeship, of a desire for immolation in the face of fire and an ending in tales of heroism, Valhalla, or on the plinth of a war memorial. However, while Samson and Harapha are brothers of 'flesh and wire' (p. 64), and notwithstanding Samson speaking of the cloud of shared identities that 'share space but in separate quarters' (p. 67),

Harapha appears to stand for an outmoded technology, a technology of simpler analogue times, FORTRAN programming language and mainframe computers, but with his God at 'his shoulder'. Harapha is also the sire of giants, creatures too big for their times, inhibited by their clumsiness while empowered by their strength. Even Goliath, the largest of his progeny, is proven a technologically outmoded device, defeated by the speed and accuracy of a boy with a sling. Nonetheless, Harapha mocks Samson and expresses scorn for his condition, finding it

> hard to resist the temptation
> to point out that your God has abandoned you
> to prison, to slavery to blindness.
> Delivered you into enemy hands!
> to paraphrase the propagandist's text. (p. 66)

The text from which the 'paraphrase' is taken is telling, for it expresses the paradox of religious belief – that Samson can be blinded and imprisoned for his service to a God that Harapha does not recognise. But Samson opens the fissure to a crucial question raised in Milton's text, the struggle over whose power should be obeyed, Dagon or Israel's God:

> *if Dagon be thy god,*
> *Go to his temple, invocate his aid*
> *With solemnest devotion, spread before him*
> *How highly it concerns his glory now*
> *To frustrate and dissolve these magic spells,*
> *Which I to be the power of Israel's God*
> *Avow, and challenge Dagon to the test,*
> *Offering to combat thee, his champion bold,*
> *With the utmost of his godhead seconded:*
> *Then thou shalt see, or rather to thy sorrow*
> *Soon feel, whose God is strongest, thine or mine.* (lines 1145-55)

To which Harapha replies:

> *Presume not on thy God. Whate'er he be,*
> *Thee he regards not,* (lines 1156-57)

Like Dalila and Samson, Harapha is also caught within a conflicted and paradoxical sensibility. He both deplores and revels in Samson's 'dire circumstances' (p. 69). But one paradox, that of religious belief, is of course already resolved in that there can be only one winner in Milton's text – and it won't be Dagon. But Kinsella's Harapha does recognise that who 'is in control / and who isn't is easily turned to / serve the triumphant' (p. 67). So, who is in control here?

The Chorus acknowledge their controlling hand in the narrative, where 'the manner of telling will / determine the reception we aim for' (p. 62). But, somebody is 'writing' the Chorus, whether Milton or Kinsella, and the Chorus ratify this in their confession of possessing a 'clear bias' (p. 61). However, another paradox is that the Chorus 'serve ourselves' as well as serving Samson. But their role is predetermined; they may comment, offer possibilities of different courses of action, but in the end they confess to not knowing the outcome – 'the future is murky' (p. 75). The Chorus shifts between then and now, between the voice of Milton and the voice of Kinsella. They also recognise that they are implicated in Samson's narrative, 'entangled' in his 'fate and death' (p. 70). They invoke the events and characters of the *Book of Judges*, of Milton's *Samson Agonistes*, and of the press and online feeds of the present, of the fields and the paddocks, the forest and the bushland. The Chorus talk of a 'girl' who speaks out against gun violence, for her 'lost classmates', her words ringing 'through myth and history and across borders / and boundaries' (p. 71). There is a clear message being expressed here, and if propaganda is not just a dirty word then this is a propaganda for positivity, for change, and 'shift', or 'shifting', is used many times in this contemporary text – 'Shift. Change. Alter.' intone the Chorus (p. 71). For the Semichorus, the command is to 'Let go. Let go. Let go.' – perhaps of such outmoded customs as vengeance, of tit-for-tat revenge killings, of the Biblical eye-for-an-eye injunction, to make some attempt to limit the vendetta. These may well be the 'shibboleths' that are invoked in the Chorus's 'Out of our shibboleths we also see' (p. 38). From a reading of the Histories of the Old Testament one could be excused for growing sickened by the litany of violence and killings, and it make sense that Samson has grown tired of this normalising of atrocities. It is enough to recall the echo from the *Book of Judges* – and the slaughter of those who cannot say the word as a password, used by the Gileadites to identify the Ephraimites, and kill them, all 42,000 of them (*Judges* XII 4-6).

There is an important reminder in here, a reminder of the endless struggle to dispense with the patterns of reciprocal retaliation, where

Shame and generations has not
Broken the ritual of killing
When it serves across time's fences' (p. 51)

Is it possible to break out of the ritual of killing? Can there be any escape from conflict? This is not the case in the 'natural' world, not in the world of plants and animals, not in the struggle for light, life, liquid. But that does not mean that conflict in any context is 'natural'. Conflicts have different contexts, and different effects. A dramatic conflict is not of the same type or scale as an armed conflict, whether with clubs or nuclear weapons.

To Conclude

Finally, the sounds of impending catastrophe invade the scene. Manoah's claims of a God who is 'served by compassion' (p. 78) are overruled by the 'sound of annihilation', a perhaps 'horrendous accident' (p. 79). Such 'horrendous accidents' are a proven fear, with echoes of Three Mile Island, and worse, Chernobyl, where 'the fallout will eat the distance / and affect friend and foe alike' (p. 80) as proofs of such fears. And Samson dies, sharing his death with those who are killed around him. But it is an act of mutual destruction – of people, but not property.

A crucial figure arrives – it is the Messenger, who plays a pivotal role in both texts – like the Messenger in Euripides'

The Bacchae and any number of classical Greek plays. The Messenger is that necessary figure who serves to describe the action off-stage. The messenger also invariably has an opinion on the events, and is often at risk of being punished for being the bringer of bad news like, among many others, the Messenger in Shakespeare's *Antony and Cleopatra* who gets slapped for his pains. This Messenger is bringing 'the facts', so the Chorus say, not the 'false news' that is so frequently called 'truth' (p. 85). The Messenger is no harbinger of good news, and the bad news is approaching – 'the fallout will eat the distance' (p. 80). The fallout is from a 'smart bomb'– a bomb that kills humans but preserves property.

Samson Agonistes was Milton's call to the English to fight against the reversal of their revolution and the restoration of a corrupt and potentially absolutist monarchy. His fear was of an obedient populace, 'by their vices brought to servitude' (line 269) who would grow

> *To love bondage more than liberty–*
> *Bondage with ease than strenuous liberty–* (lines 270-1)

As Manoah laments, the problem is that 'we are enemies to ourselves, / that we are enemy to life outside / our own, and so often to our own lives' (p. 86). Kinsella's Semichorus warns of an echo of a blindness to what freedom might be, of a 'turning off from reality' like the Israelites of Milton's dramatic poem, and the English of Milton's time who 'chose to recall the exiled King from France',[8] and where participation 'is sold as a hashtag on devices / that extract the heart of the country' (p. 85). In our enthrallment to our electronic devices, the internet, movies, sport, television, celebrity gossip, have we grown to love bondage more than liberty? And in this state of what passes for happy bondage, is the thinking of liberty too 'strenuous' to be contemplated?

[8] Bennett, 228.

The Chorus warn us in closing, if we are searching for resolution or catharsis, then look elsewhere. Kinsella does not project a wistful and forlorn hope that things will necessarily change, notwithstanding the best efforts of those, including poets, who might strive and fight for something better. We are all caught within the paradox of a wish for life, and so often a careless urge towards destruction, whether of the self, society, or the planet. But that is no reason to give up the fight, not to continue to explore the nature of the paradox, even though all things may seem to conspire against it. But the answer is not in what the Chorus has to say, and we should never trust this Chorus. Seek elsewhere for resolution, and keep searching.

WORKS CITED
Barker, Howard. 'Judith. A Parting from the Body.' *Howard Barker. Collected Plays 3*. London: Calder, 1996. 241–66.
Bennett, Joan S. 'A reading of Samson Agonistes.' Danielson, Dennis, ed. *The Cambridge Companion to Milton*. CUP, 1989. 225–241.
Dylan, Bob. 'Tombstone Blues.' Witmark & Son, USA, 1965.
Hone, Ralph E., ed. *John Milton's Samson Agonistes: The Poem and Materials for Analysis*. Scranton, Penn.: Chandler Publishing Company, 1966. 97-103.
Radzinowicz, Mary Ann. *Toward Samson Agonistes*. Princeton, NJ: Princeton Univ. Press, 1978.

SAMSON AGONISTES
An intertextual re-dramatisation after Milton

by John Kinsella

*I relied on her charms to get me through
a foreign land.*

from 'Killing Delilah' by Tracy Ryan

THE PERSONS

Samson
Manoa the father of Samson
Dalila his wife
Harapha of Gath
Publick Officer
Messenger

THE ARGUMENT

Which version of a story are we being privileged to hear? Which version is this? And told with what emphasis, what distractions, what purpose? What are the agendas behind its telling? Milton's Samson is naturally a piece of propaganda. But why and how? Well, here it is intertextually retold. The narrative is similar if the scene-setting both more generic and more specific. This is a tale of conflicted belief, values, and desires. It is a paradox in which other paradoxes multiply. It undoes ownership, nation, systems of control, the primacy of the human over nature, and especially militarism. It is a pacifist text in which dispossessions are confronted. It is a pacifist text in which denials and exclusions are confronted. It advocates equality, egalitarianism, gender liberation, gender justice, a flexibility of identity, and respect for different belief systems. The story is told – Samson, destroyer of an army, is blinded and enslaved. He considers his position in conversation with his father, with others of his community, and with his wife Dalila whom he blames for his downfall, the robbing of his strength (embodied in his hair, which is dead cells) through betrayal. But Samson's bonding with 'the other', the 'foreign', is also a path to fairness and justice.

And it is in this that we find Samson deviating from the role expected of him. As Crass once said, 'Big Man, Big M.A.N… develop your muscles, use your prick like a gun…' Well, Samson becomes aware. He also becomes aware that he had been used as a violent extension of the state. Not a specific state, but all states. Samson here is lifted out of cultural, ethnic and spatial specificity to become symbol. But as the narrative unravels, symbol and event become 'confused'. Samson does not intend the violence on the gathered crowd, the crowd gathered to relish his servitude, but cannot control the violence that has been instilled in him. The pillars are symbols of a nuclear accident – or rather, maybe, a dirty bomb, or a radiation leak. There's a witness, but he leaves the scene knowing something ill will happen, and watches via camera from a distance. Samson, after all, is a cyborg – how much of him is human anyway? What are the rights of AI and what are the God-particle motives for creating it? It's complex, and sometimes contradictory, and the text attempts to confront this, and the limitations of creative textual conventions. What is it saying, and what has happened? The damaging of people is a brutal conceit for the damaging of the biosphere whose death is death of us all – total death. This is a text of pacifist resistance, against ownership and profit, against possession and exclusion. It suggests a redistribution and faith that's diverse, intact, and anti-colonial. It suggests, it reports, it struggles with the machinery of state, company and media. It is inside the fake news it tries to undo. It knows the devices and infrastructure of information are a paradox that damage as much as heal, and that there is a cost to the planet. A paradox machine that seeks to be organic, to breathe, to be part of without excluding. What it does know is that the arms industry serves only death, and only its own desires for wealth, control, and deletion to increase itself: it is the endgame, it is only death, nothing more.

THE SCENE BEFORE THE PRISON IN GAZA

SAMSON: We find places where we might relieve our
condition – a bonding to devices
we worship, the medium of a freedom
that reverses sun and shade, liberties
of the moment that make the air and soil
toxic for us all. And here is mine, this
grove of remnant vegetation, deep roots
reaching below the winter creek, butcher
birds imitating the sound of death's machines.
But let me rest here to regain my feet,
to let the smell of eucalyptus make taste
on this bitten tongue. This inland catchment.
But this day is the sea people's feast day,
a day of worshipping sun, sand and fun.
Many sea creatures will be sacrificed.
A nation's self-defining holiday
whereby making even their enemy
work would affront their patriotism.
And so I rest beneath great flooded gums,
but so easily prey to what has been,
what I have been part of – conflict, warfare,
Superhornets, Migs, hypersonic nukes.
It falls so easily from the texting tongue.
This weaponised self, this cyborg proto-
type that is me guided by angels, drone
operators who go home to above
average income lifestyle church and state
lifestyles. I am a child of them all, of
all people who fuse with technology:
of fire and metal, of pathfinding
for artificial intelligence: for
making life for profit-sake, Rocket X,
car on mars, nerve agents, God particles
and particulates. So out of my

ego distress, out of my programming,
out of sleeper agent conditioning,
I start to wonder to which God structure
I belong – designed for mass destruction,
for such a fait accompli destiny –
I start to wonder why I am left here
to perish: betrayed, captured and blinded,
made a mockery of by my enemies,
put on display on their Facebook accounts,
to grind grain under their pitiless gaze.
I see them in my mind's eye, a spectacle
of hate exchange, provoking by 'roid rage
which simmers in this bestial displacement.
I question what it is I am supposed
to deliver, what the birds, marsupials,
insects and fresh water crustaceans plead
of me. Saboteur, they seem to whisper,
and I strain hard against this calm, cool, shade –
eyeless in Gaza, bonded to labour
in non-binary community
with other slaves. But pause, take stock, and make
another script that doesn't appropriate
the suffering of others – God's creatures
as I question God, all schematics, all
scheme, all masterplans gone awry, all
chaos I look to for derivation:
rather, I should this hate on myself,
take these questions and displace my own greed.
And then there's woman blame, there's that gender
game I've been conditioned into. I see
it now, as gender cascades out of my
prison, my imprisonment, the shackles
we've all had to deal with. I now see that
speaking my secret was deep liberty –
power sharing. I am not ashamed
of a sensitivity to tears, and won't
back engineer my one epiphany.

I ceded power – what is strength without
sharing, without acknowledging lack?
I was a child of the 60s and wore
my hair long, and did not cut when fashion
demanded – of that I am still proud. But
when it came to passing through court, wanting
to travel across borders, I complied
to make traversal easier. Never
again. Fashion is the tool of tyrants.
But peace – forgiveness is never finite,
and though blindness is pain it is also
gain, opening a world empathy
and sensation I had been insensitive
to. But to be chained and enslaved is never
acceptable, and I say this inside
out – that the light that has been made extinct
to me is the light of hope, is the light
of living beyond capitalist lust,
beyond profiteers always enemies
of the people, wherever they come from.
The vilest excel me – mining and oil
executives, land developers, arms
manufacturers, the NRA – they
creep and yet 'see' while seeing nothing, fraud
their guiding light, thieves of the secular
and sacred, marketing equality
only to increase their markets, caring
nothing for culture or difference outside
sales diversity. But I am the fool
to be so readily deployed and used
by their offices. The self's paradox:
in power of others, never in my own;
scarce half I seem to live, dead more than half.
o dark, dark, dark, amid the blaze of noon,   80
irrecoverably dark, total Eclipse
without all hope of day!
Singularity, easy obsession

of now – our God, the new physics, 'knowledge'
a tool to sidetrack all alternative
knowledges. Empirical desire where
metaphor isn't light,
and light is to be reached,
a marker of conquest
as the Wizard of Oz is to the Dark
Side of the Moon. How many units
of the soul have been sold?
Such retina display fixation,
such embodying identity in
an orb so delicate – they send in their
probes to fix your soul's metadata, shop
you to the highest bidder in your search
for the best possible deal. A living death.
A veil of freedom you'd vote in death for.
These games of light and graves, threats of exile
from self-belief, shame you into darkness.
Buried yet not exempt.
Out of body wastes a reclamation –
DNA profiling attaching
us to heritage, once again
a liberty to exclude
others – to make an othering.
This patenting of life.
Denying massacres
are living history, are all our failure
to know the sacredness of life, all life.
But who comes here? I hear many feet make
their way across contested ground. Do they
come to mock me, take a selfie, report
my fate in the *Guardian* to increase
their following, appease their guilt, smite their
enemies and alleviate a doubt?

CHORUS: There he is – take it carefully,
let us not surprise him – painful
it is to see him so distressed, languid,
his body shapeless and abandoned
by his will – the great resister
brought down to the level
of dirt. Surely it's not really
him – who paused the slaughter
by standing between all warring
peoples, who stood up for
the lion and respected
the jawbone of the ass,
who was one with the hive
and yet to be held accountable
as individual, as *person* –
ran on embattelld Armies clad in Iron,
and weaponless himself,
made Arms ridiculous, useless the forgery
of brazen shield and spear, the hammer'd Cuirass,
Chalybean temper'd steel, and frock of mail
Adamantean Proof;
but safest he who stood aloof –
who refused warcraft, who refused
to value one life over another!
And as he stood between the armies
of the modern world,
as he said we are all
one people and united we
stand, divided we fall,
he said that all we can afford
to learn from history
is decency, not methods of killing.
And he used his prodigious strength to part
wave after wave of self-aggrandisement,
the generals and captains of industry
watching from highground, via satellites,
making strategy and tactics pictures

on their Instagram accounts (set *private*),
Heaven their secret weapon, the fake news
bonanza live newsfeed entertainment.
All those points on the map
geolocated as
Pokémon destinations, Nintendo's
global venture which Renga we
might all join without the risk taking
more than we went in with?
Augmented reality is a gift
of corporate world building with cultural
intactness? Any more than an Anglo-
Canadian-French-American or
Indian mining venture making giant holes
in land stolen from those indigenous
peoples who refuse to comply.
Samson was just saying –
intactness is as complex as
capitalism let us say.
But not for me today!
But that was back then,
when he ranged outside their
range. And now they have made
a darkness of darkness, taken
away even liberties of blindness.
You have become, Samson, trapped inside self
you resisted – what of your deep belief
that all difference could be celebrated,
that Palestine and Israel can exist
as one without the hierarchy of land
owned by anyone. The land 'owns' us all!
But let him know that we
keep the faith – that his strength
is more than symbol, and more than brute force –
it is a weaving of the organic
and inorganic – a cosmology!

SAM: *I hear the sound of words, their sense the air*
Dissolves unjointed e're it reach my ear.

CHOR: He speaks. Come, closer now. A permission
almost given by one who has had his
right to give permission taken from him.
His massive body is opposition
to imperialism and yet also
subtexted by residues of the same.
He writhes with contradictions, looking for
a way to illumination. We must
soothe his wounds with an open mindedness.

SAM: That fact that you come to me when I am
at my lowest speaks volumes for your love
and friendship – I am accused of holding
aggressive and appropriative views
I barely recognise. It is not people
I oppose but their 'leaders', exploiters
who sell themselves as caring. Corporate
enslavement – in that sweatshop shoes are turned
out to be sold in the community
of those who die to make them. Paradox?
The machine, friends, is designed out of these.
I have blinded myself to suffering
in others by suffering myself.
I have become Timon of Athens who
himself came of me – a temporal loop.
Now I am getting things in perspective,
in proportion – I am expendable
and seeing is a luxury I don't
warrant. The lampooning and ridicule,
the plays of wit that bring perpetrators
their just reward – accolades from poets,
are neither here nor there as biosphere

collapse rounds out our inequalities.
Women were short-strawed by God and then left
to hang out the washing. To share fairness
across genders is the message I think
you are conveying. I see slant now, so
maybe I am wilfully reshaping.
Sandy Hook really happened. Don't forget!

CHOR: It's in your favour you stepped out of 'race'
constraints, made ecumenical your love.
That you recognise patriarchy has
dissolved the bonds of trust, fairness, and truth.
That you take the blame for all of us on
your shoulders. We'd be hypocrites to say
otherwise, though we are hypocrites in
saying so – the social organism!

SAM: Marriage outside permission, outside those
conventions which have kept us under thumb.
Yes, *I did it my way*. And now I pay?
So, why undo what has been written before –
maybe so we neither have to censor
the original or simply ignore
entirely because it is no longer
acceptable to contemporary
sensibilities – though metaphor will
always evade the shifts of time being
made from the fraying threads of time itself.
I have sought not to oppress oppressors
but disarm and make them ineffective.
Out of the Avon Valley I have seen
the far right groups celebrating their love
made of bigotry, those bonds of such hate
that corellas flee in flocks from such looks.
But now, out of sight, I see clearer

than ever that silence or internal
anguish is a wedding band to hatred.
I spoke out and the CIA yoked with
the Australian intelligence forces
got me – pacifism a deadly threat.

CHOR: Provocation – what is its true nature?
Israel and Palestine meet at a place
which knows no boundaries. Their languages speak
across divides and make songs of all life.

SAM: Fault can be distributed among us
all. All. It's a motif of the flower
in the desert. The peace poem – I don't
need acknowledgement as acknowledgement
undoes the act. Yes, the deeds speak louder
than the dooer, but many won't listen
no matter how ready the evidence.
Wars break out because we all engender
warlike behaviour in our children – we
sell such violence as part of the human
condition they will one day have to face
up to, we think ratings on movies will
filter, make 'age appropriate' when all
violence feeds violence. Blind utopia?
A vision outside what you term 'normal'.
I reject that notion entirely. The
harass of the land is the bulldozer
is the killing of ancient trees which
harbour entire ecosystems, it is
the plasticated oceans, it is the
fallout from reactors, it is the spray
billowing over crops and plants called weeds
emerging from the cracks in concrete, it
is the preying on genitalia.

We implicate through our mere existence.
What chance? For me, ignorance is not bliss.
Nations will grow corrupt because they are
nations. Nations are nations because they
seek to empower at someone's expense.
God has expanded catchment for all –
each and every one of us contributes
to the imprint, the footprint on its face.
I praise the poetry of 'stony wastes',
I praise the poetry of lush spaces,
I praise the poetry of difference,
I praise poetry of co-existence.

CHOR: Your words of remembrance break the strains
of prosody's conventions. Remember
water-boarding in Iraq and the spawn
of terrorism, remember the lies
of Guantanamo Bay, remember the
'coalition' bombing Syria then
superpower rivalry over bones
of civilisation, semiotics
of death and victory and 'safeguarding'
interests. Remember refugees
turned back at borders, lost to the blue sea.
Out of our shibboleths we also see.
Many of us speak against *all* forms of death.

SAM: We are so much closer to each other
than we are allowed to think – God alone
does not make life, we make and take life, too.

CHOR: *Just are the ways of God,*
and justifiable to Men;
unless there be who think not God at all,

if any be, they walk obscure;
for of such Doctrine never was there School,
but the heart of the Fool,
and no man therein Doctor but himself.
But there are exceptions… yes, we admit.
Astonished? To take out the conflict is
to render the narrative 'impotent'?
Rethink the tale, rethink the storyboard –
the visuals compel us to listen.
Think of the billabong, think of wetlands
alive with ibises and night herons.
Think of mosses and lichens clustering
narrow mountain paths on the other side
of the world. Think the optimism of
the scorpion in desert sands, and think
the oasis. Think the rich life of ghosts
we deprive of futures with our toxic
wastes, think of the glories
of permaculture, of
village-scale existence.
Freedom on another's
terms is rarely freedom
at all – we keep this in mind as we speak
collectively – responsibility
is to support but not to incite you
to reject what you've come
to learn through suffering, joining the pain
of so many others persecuted
by states. Law best fits place,
and not twisted to draw
others into its circumference who have
known other zones and other responses.
These are tangled moralities, and how to
admit us all and respect exceptions
is beyond this gathering of shared but
different voices. But now comes an old
man with flowing white hair – yes, your father,

Manoah. How should we best receive him?

SAM: Hearing of his approach doesn't make it
easier – I confront my pain again.

MANOAH: *O miserable change! is this the man,*
that invincible Samson, far renown'd,
as a weapon we old folk could deploy
against our enemies, comply to our
lethal ways. Son, son! You were an army
in yourself! Born but altered to best serve
the state – what a shimmering sacrifice.
Your angel skills gave you rockstar status –
what more could a father or offspring want?
And you came as such a gift when we thought
barrenness a punishment, but who would
take my lot given how things have ended?
Why did God take my prayers reroute them
into torment. Why make the skyscraper
only to topple it with an earthquake?
I will think of God's beneficence in
what you were rather than what you now are.

SAM: Filial duty leads me to shoulder
your words on already weighted shoulders,
but they are no easier to take though
I'd shift blame elsewhere to alleviate
the distress you've fuelled. But still, I take blame.
I cannot escape my class, my gender,
the privilege with which I boost my harsh
protest. So… *I myself have brought them on,*
sole Author I, sole cause: if aught seem vile,
as vile hath been my folly, who have profan'd
the mystery of God giv'n me under pledge,

then it has been letting my maleness ease
a path through life while knowing it was wrong.
Further, though I called no one enemy
I took the hurts I thought they'd dispensed me
and quietly thought them enemy – this has
consequences to self and the cause's
integrity. I want to say mea
culpa, but I am conflicted, feeling
aggrieved and humble at once, lashing out
mentally at failed relationships, at
bullies and capitalists who have traced
my footsteps across the supermarket
aisles. I mean, getting to the point, the she –
Dalila – asked me to share my power
but I played games with her, enticing sex
as exchange, fooling myself the pleasure
was mutual, that I was a generous
lover. It's embarrassing to say this,
and fathers want to think of their sons as
conquerors, as chips off the old block, as
catches. I know I called it betrayal
when she revealed my vanity – the thing
I'd accused her of day after day – but
it wasn't all one way. She called out my
wiles. Truth is, I was in search of comfort
which costs the ear that has to bear it – we
rather than me was the variable
I missed, failed my own effeminacy,
played my manliness for all it was worth.
She who'd been my bond slave said enough is
enough. My blindness had nothing to do
with the loss of my eyesight – I had served
patriarchy while claiming I was not
doing so. Ignominious. Infamous.
The grinding of flour, making of bread,
the serving of man by woman will end.
Slavery must end in its many forms.

MAN: And so the father would have his son
in his own image but both less and more –
and so the sensitivities are stamped
out or rerouted, are channelled into
a form the father 'can be proud of'. But
I admit to not seeing how it might go,
as if your membership of another
party might really be a deceit that serves
our mutual interest – get inside to break
down the enemy's confidence, to serve
our father's father's fathers. Keep all wealth
and power flowing through bloodlines, captives
of eugenics and property, of arms.
The smalls arms company I have built up
from a legacy is the bright future
of our family – no woman or 'them'
is going to undo our destiny:
we have worked tradition and religion
and nation and history to our own
ends – and now you run the risk of letting
it all fall, of your lippy and indy
stance re liberty make a fairness that's
not fair to us. Temptation is social
and giving ground to make up difference.
You shame me. But still, here you are in chains,
here you are broken by a reflection
of our own company – they love women
and 'them' and others no more than we do,
they just want our market share, to sell arms
and call it job production, to make it
normal, as natural as sliced bread, as
democratic as a sports team in form.
The worst of it is that this very day
our rivals are celebrating your loss
to us, your capitulation, giving
thanks to their God Dagon that you are
no longer slaughtering them. I won't

unpick the logic because I can see
you're not up to it, but just think of that
idolatrous and blaspheming lot
whooping it up at your – my – our – expense!
All that glitz, all those cameras – and the cost
to the firm to mine user data to
make it all okay again. A nightmare!
Sure, we'd do the same if the shoe was on
the other foot, but it's no time for jokes.
Samson, of all thy sufferings think the heaviest,
of all reproach the most with shame that ever
could have befall'n thee and thy Fathers house.

SAM: Father, I admit I have brought you shame,
I admit that Dagon will be glorified
as a result of my failure, but I
don't admit I've brought scandal to Israel.
I want nothing to do with weaponry.
I didn't kill anyone. The board – and
you – have turned me into propaganda.
I care for the people of Gaza and
don't reduce their God to a lesser God
than ours. We share a sense of God, we
share a biosphere, a solar system,
a physics and a metaphysics. They
are brothers and sisters and others who
struggle for peace against the violence
of their leaders, against patriarchy
in its many, shape-shifting forms. You, too,
call me cyborg because I don't fit with that
model constructed out of 'destiny' –
well, I write eternity in this
darkness which is allowing me to see.
God and Dagon are what we make of them.
Give them both peace and growth and tolerance
and they will find ways to converse, to share

our love. Don't look at me like that, as if
I am anathema – this hippy hair
you pretended was strength! I know how much
it embarrassed you, that I found lovers
of all genders rewarding. I am no trophy
for your way of life. I worship freedom
but not as an extension of the state!

MAN: I am a man of action. I control
a powerful multinational arms
manufacturing company. I have
the best legal minds at my beck & call,
protecting mutual interests.
I can call God on the phone anytime
and HIS response will be swift… effective.
But even so, I have opened channels
of communication with the warlords
of the opposition and discussed
terms for your release, offered a ransom.
I am hoping they will have extracted
enough propaganda value from you
to sign off and forget all about you.

SAM: *Spare that proposal, Father, spare the trouble
of that sollicitation; let me here,
as I deserve, pay on my punishment;
and expiate, if possible, my crime,
shameful garrulity. To have reveal'd
secrets of men, the secrets of a friend,*
but not the one's people think I've betrayed.
Rather, I have said 'peace' and profited
from the arms trade – the way it filters
down through family, through society.
When the minister and businessman work
together to manufacture small arms,

or naval vessels, to boost Australia
(say… say) to the TOP TEN of arms dealers,
then you get the picture. In all of this,
as citizen-son I am complicit.
Loose lips sink ships, but they also cover
up crimes of ease and comfort in the face
of most brutal grievous wrong. Fruits of abyss.

MAN: I am still a parent. I look for your
contrition but am contrite myself – wrong
is a complex array, and I am deep inside it.
God is more flexible and more… more than
I care to admit. This is confronting
at the most confronting of times – death
nearby illuminates the death we make.
Country is more than administration.
Country is much more than the company.
Country is not an idea of power
but a strength in itself that needs respect
in terms of its dirt and growth and lifeforce.
Maybe these are ingredients of prayer.
To lose you. To hear truths I cannot bear.
What is prayer? Where have my prayers been going?

SAM: So, we begin to share and understand
at the point of despair, when all seems lost.
But really, my arrogance has been my
downfall. So obsessed with the heroic,
preening as I was praised, product of my
own publicity, chest to pin medals
on – though I blame you for what I became
I admit to agency. I liked praise
and prizes, the authority that comes
with victory – a voluptuous life.
But I won't buy into shifting the blame

to the woman, calling her concubine,
who shore me like a tame Wether, while sheep
fall to the killer's blade, where life is weighed
and apportioned different value – disarmed
is the lamb to slaughter. My hair was *shed.*

CHOR: It's so easy to be lured by the 'good
things' in life – to take the light while it glows
and indulge through the night, to accept light
made by damaging country – mines and wastes:
quick fix radioactive legacy.

SAM: I partied. I grew addicted to fast
drugs, to slow drugs, to a polyphonous
mix of experiences: sounds and sight
ran together, I created havoc
yet was fast to blame others, not myself.

CHOR: *O madness, to think use of strongest wines*
and strongest drinks our chief support of health,
when God with these forbid'n made choice to rear
his mighty Champion, strong above compare,
whose drink was only from the liquid brook.

SAM: I work things awry, I make no sense
of my contradictory nature. I take
down the fences to let all life pass through,
and yet make fences to block out those who
see life differently from me. Now under
the yoke, crushed and cut off from the lighting
I've known as illumination, I shift
ground from beneath my own invisible

feet. I know the identity I have
till now denied is speaking via me,
but I obfuscate and side step, careful
not to be construed as 'effeminate'.
And yet, here I am bonded with others
who had no rights no acclamation no
freedom to speak of – we share the same fate?
It's easy to give in now, welcome
an end to pain when I've had such leisure.

MAN: So what, you'll just give in? I might not be
in a position to speak from moral
highground, but flawed as I now admit
I am, it seems ridiculous in terms
of your hard-gained self-awareness to let
friend or foe obliterate you. To serve
them is to serve servility itself,
to condemn fellow slaves to slavery.
You have a gift of insight, you can see
your own flaws, you know things have to be changed.
Think of the beauty of the world you let
pass by with little thought beyond the show,
and reinvisage it as life itself!

SAM: Nothing is as it seems. I am dizzy
with the changes. Who are you? What am I?
I am haunted by the doubts of action,
and the bright spaces of forest are gone
because I've cleared it to dirt. All light now is
lightless, a darkness doubled and doubled
again. I feel nothing for 'successes'
as in achieving them I denatured –
only my weaponised body, devoid
of institutional guidance systems,

persists, flying blind I have run my race,
left high and dry and dead in the water,
unravelling into self-parody.

MAN: A father faced with his own absurd
trajectory either signs off or tries
to recover some of what's been lost. My
renouncing arms doesn't make their arms right!
Healing words are all I have to offer.

SAM: *O that torment should not be confin'd*
to the bodies wounds and sores
with maladies innumerable
in heart, head, brest, and reins;
but must secret passage find
to th' inmost mind,
but speak out through my actions and values,
as of my spirits they are made.
How easily as 'man of
the world' I have gained the limelight,
and now a hostage am quickly
forgotten. But my grief is not
grief for myself alone, as it's
not possible to be alone
among the ghosts of extinction.
All those murdered are with us now,
and forgetting is what allows
the murdering to keep on happening.
Tormentors of people are armed
with deadly stings, and tormentors
of other life are armed with speech –
the excuse before bulldozers
clear a way for 'civilising',
where 'development' is seen as
time, and 'progress' seen as an end

in itself. Such calibrations
of occupation, such desire
to remove a neighbour – we are
all in this together, rising
seas a declaration inland
as a post-exploration re-
bound. And the cooling herbs we take
from jungles where different life
goes on, soon tilt the stockmarket,
then development says jungle
begone – in the contradiction
we struggle with inflamed despair
and sense of Heav'ns desertion.
I was his nursling once and choice delight,
his destin'd from the womb,
promisd by Heavenly message twice descending.
When my mother and my father
are not allowed responsibility,
I – preordained, predestined, constructed –
roll off the AI production line. I –
evil and good and trending and hashtagged.
I – no petition can save me
from what they – you all! — have manufactured.

CHOR: It's a time for peaceful but remorseless
resistance – we should be speaking out how
ever we can without immediately
lapsing back into our complacency,
into enjoying the fruits of wrong
while condemning the wrong that made
them – dissembling, apportioning blame
when we are taking what we can get.
God of our Fathers, what is man!
Such contrariness in the face of
the tempest we have patented.
Such contrariness in the face of

a rufous whistler singing
soft-loud, speaking to migrating
birds overflying – all welcome,
free movement, but acknowledgement
of ancient connection to country – land
that is a circulatory system,
that is body itself. And as the lost
wash up on these shores we welcome them home
because a home is both fixed and shifting.
All versions of God are acceptable,
all beliefs to be respected, but such
machinery of intolerance has
no place in these angelic orders.
We're shifting the variables.
In your misery we celebrate an
awareness which fair community –
which scrambles the haves and have nots,
which lets the seasons in all their
difference retain local autonomy,
integrity, intactness. All peoples'
safety, all persons' safety, all living
creatures matching time to the right of breath.
The success of the AK47s
in reaching battlefields was not a source
of pride in the end. But the inventing
was the first step to annihilation.
Knowledge doesn't grow from products,
too grievous for the trespass or omission,
oft leav'st them to the hostile sword
while making swords themselves and calling them
'defence' — a short circuiting of logic,
short change in the capitalists' coffers.
Down in the Hills there's an old man
who pays his son to shoot rare white-
tailed black cockatoos as they land
on his fruit trees – he sees this
as the right of the orchardist.

Shame and generations have not
broken the ritual of killing
when it serves across time's fences.
Instead, through you, Samson, we grow
aware of our own limitations, our
desire to control the fabric of our
'society' — by which we mean exclusion.
There are so many subtle ways
of pretending we're broad minded
but closing the door – you are shouldering
responsibility, earthing our lies.
It served us you going into battle.
A standing army 'doing its duty'.
Our dirty work, but enjoying the power.
The old grey poet and contradiction?
Why didn't he call for abolition!
You are not at a loss with
a 'disability', you have
a quality of insight – the loss is in the control
both the enemy and, truth be told, *we*
exerted over you – expectation.
The problem is in the word 'champion'
in so many ways – we replace it with
Samson, your name. You are *real* and *also*
symbolise poverty, sickness, disease
only because of what is being forced
on you, as you too enforced on others.
But who is this, what thing of Sea or Land?
femal of sex it seems,
that so bedeckt, ornate, and gay,
comes this way sailing
like a stately Ship
of Tarsus, bound for th' Isles
of Javan or Gadier
with all her bravery on, and tackle trim,
sails fill'd, and streamers waving,
courted by all the winds that hold them play,

an Amber sent of odorous perfume
her harbinger, a damsel train behind;
some rich Philistian Matron she may seem,
and now at nearer view, no other certain
than Dalila thy wife.

SAM: I am supposed to refuse her but what
time have we for dramatic irony?

CHOR: We could describe her attire, set the 'scene'
for reception. We could track 'feminine'
qualities to set her as some men would
set her. But that's sexism and we know it,
so why pretend otherwise for the sake
of an audience's delectation?
She is weeping and she wishes to speak.

DALILA: I am here though I dread your displeasure,
Samson. This stacking of blame for a failed
relationship – this distaff to your spear
I rejected, I still reject, but
I am here, foreshadowing a shift
in the power balance or overtly
leaving myself open to your disdain,
your anger. But I don't take loyalty
as lightly as you claim, and your blaming
is what brings these tears, not blank contrition.
Takes two to tango, partner, and we have
to own our assured mutual destruction –
that tragic joke of acronyms, title
deeds dished out to humans. I have shared with
my culture, lit up a foreign beauty.

Sam: I want to break you, abuse you, take
my revenge, but know that my self-hate drives
this pathology. A dead catharsis.
Every time I took you for myself, love-
talk to ease my way, get what pleasured me...
to break all faith, all vows, deceive, betray,
then as repentant to submit, beseech,
and reconcilement move with feign'd remorse,
confess, and promise wonders in my *change,*
not truly penitent – I don't blame you
if you see my volte face in such a light.
You have entangled with a poisonous
snake and been bitten – constrict the poison!

Dal: So why is it I feel compelled to beg
your forgiveness? Why do I take a back
seat. Hear me, Samson, don't play binary
explanations because they don't exist,
never existed outside the construct
you helped elevate on your massive
shoulders. There's a body of literature
to be absorbed through the skin, and it is
not cut off from you. Now is the time for
redistribution, for letting gardens
be, for ending the colonisations.
Was it not weakness also to make known
for importunity, that is for naught,
wherein consisted all thy strength and safety?
But I am not switch hitting, not shifting
a blame: I can reverse words in my mouth:
To what I did thou shewdst me first the way
and apply them to your speech cartouche, too!
Whatever you say, I know you still think,
deep down beyond critique, that I am flawed,
that 'frailty' made me betray you – untrue!
I loved you beyond gender and beyond

surveillance, I loved you without a care
for popular opinion – I love all
peoples but love persons, too. All censorship
is anathema to me. You forget
my body beyond the sensual gifts
you think it bestows on you – if I give,
I give, it's not a supermarket of
flesh and sensations, a making of *you*!
Your journey of self-discovery, of
genius, of creativity, all
expressed through an ideal of the 'female'.
I saw thee mutable! All of 'us' so
expendable on your journey, that old trick
of 'wanderer' and 'individual' —
keeper of secrets, possessor of those
eureka! moments like a quota of
appropriated eggs. Enterprising,
intrepid, faced with endless temptation –
O the trials and tribulations of your
patriarchal bullshit. Robes of power.
Did you for a moment think of what
it was like stuck at home, locked into your
fantasy, an intelligence held back
by firewalls you alone could never
design – but rather, an entire gang
of your corrupt mates conspiring… their snares!
And what you don't seem to get is that through
this I loved you and still love you – it makes
no sense but it's real. And I love across
cultures not to diminish but enhance!
Be not unlike all others, not austere
as thou art strong, inflexible as steel.
if thou in strength all mortals dost exceed,
in uncompassionate anger do not so.

SAM: *How cunningly the sorceress displays*
her own transgressions, to upbraid me mine!
I am drawn to say this, however wrong
I know it to be – a default setting.
But I say it and retract it, this drive
to contradiction that defines presence.
I entangle myself in shame to shift
blame, and redefine a criminal code.
I torment myself with truth, and yet take
truth out of truth to make it easier
for me to bear. Wallow in my self-blame.
This darkness is not sleep, but awareness.
I can see a map clearly, but will not
follow it. I call it imperialist
and yet have every trade route memorised.
Metaphor excuses and makes my love –
the snake is the rhizome that feeds the tree,
and I cannot unravel evidence.
I cannot relinquish hate. I am trapped.

DAL: As I have been by issues of loyalty,
as I have been by the machinations
of nation and class, gender and duty.
All those ropes binding me, pulling on me
as these chains enravel you now. Alone?
No, we are bound together in our lack.
Religion can console and give direction
but it can also bring despair and leave
us disorientated – we serve with
belief and humility to have our
faith turned against us. But it doesn't have
to be this way – belief without control
is possible and each of us decides
the right and wrong of the situation.
The authorities – both religious and
secular – would manipulate who we

are to suit their endgame. Let's stand outside
to best serve inside. If to *public good
private respects must yield*, then also let
public good yield to the private as well.
Authority is not justice – it
*took full possession of me and prevail'd;
Vertue, as I thought, truth, duty so enjoyning* –
but now I unmake to live and let live.

SAM: We all feign religion to justify
our position – an easy hypocrisy.
Which is not to say one shouldn't respect
belief or worship, but be wary re
how it can be manipulated – faith
can kill, but faith can liberate without
harm. Remember, though I could have played it
safe and chosen a bride from among my
own, I chose you – of another culture,
of foreign ways, of experiences
beyond my own. I chose unfamiliar
territory. I chose outside knowledge.

DAL: Sorry, but I have to interrupt your
self-praise! My body does not translate or
transcribe into territory or 'choice'!
You forget, 'husband', I also stepped out
beyond my safety zone, outside a 'deal'!

SAM: And I trusted you and shared such secrets
that undermined not only me but my
people – maybe that's the crime of marriage.

Dal: It doesn't have to be a bargain of
inequality, but I need to live
outside the rules of society – to
answer to each other… rather, rather…

Sam: These espionage ploys, these sleeper cells,
this body made in the image of MAN,
this OMO DEI, this nation and country
slippage, this enemy and ally, this
planting of trees to carbon credit while
demolishing telescope array size chunks
of bush to speak radiation, this law
of nature to undo nature, this chip
through which I opened doors to the inner
sanctum, now useless embedded in my
skin, this barcode tattoo across my chest,
these parents, these friends – associates, these
new *men conspiring to uphold thir state*
by worse than hostile deeds, violating the ends
for which our countrey is a name so dear;
Will our Gods recognise us, the mist of
electromagnetic radiation spread
through the network of phone masts like heaven?

Dal: *In argument with men a woman ever*
goes by the worse, whatever be her cause,
you'd like to think, but I too can argue
semantics, take maths to theology.

Sam: It is hard for me to process outside
the circumstances you now find me in.

DAL: *I was a fool, too rash, and quite mistaken*
in what I thought would have succeeded best.
Let me obtain forgiveness of thee, Samson,
afford me place to shew what recompence –
but don't get me wrong, I do not intend
to go on hands and knees to my people
or yours asking forgiveness for what is
not to forgive – difference, resistance
to the status quo – but rather the means
to ends is questionable, and aggression
serves no God effectively or justly.
I am complicit in loving you, but love
is not a choice, though never doubt it has
a politics. But punishing you in
this way, confining you to a prison
of torture and torment, occluding sight
that sightlessness might bring by denying
hope is war beyond warfare – reflecting
no faith outside the blankness of conquest.
I would release you from this death sentence.
I would claim life against a force majeure.

SAM: *No, no, of my condition take no care;*
it fits not; thou and I long since are twain;
let's not go through this all over again –
I want nothing from you, I have nothing
to give. You would raise me up to watch me
fall again. Which is not to deny love,
but to deny my own complicit
nature – accept that I used you to climb
the ladder of self-esteem, reinforce
my masculinity. 'Sorceress' is
the leitmotif, though I know its
emptiness. The language gives me tools
as it reflects the values of control.
This antiphrasis I am caught within,

ploys of rhetoric designed to keep
upper ground when the field is lost – I am
trapped within a militarised discourse.
Torment! I say you will betray me yet
again because I know betrayal has been
written into the social contract, but
not as I am suggesting to save face.
God is watching this performance, this show
of life drawing to a bitter end.
This Gaol I count the house of Liberty
to thine whose doors my feet shall never enter.

DAL: What self-indulgent crap, Samson. Here you
speak as others also suffer on death
row – this slavery is massive and feeds
the wealth of a world to extract
everything it can from the downtrodden.
Let me approach at least, and touch thy hand.

SAM: If that happens I will be torn apart
by conflicting emotions – I will die
over and over while I still breathe, and
a magnesium flash will light up darkness
with such intensity my strength will be
called out. I was conditioned not to show
'weakness' by family and schooling, on
the sports and battle fields. If your skin should
touch my skin again it will be as lightning –
death within death, fall within fall: shock, awe!
Burnt out memories. No! No! No! *Farewell!*

DAL: *I see thou art implacable, more deaf*
to prayers, then winds and seas, yet winds to seas
are reconcil'd at length, and Sea to Shore:

thy anger, unappeasable, still rages,
eternal tempest never to be calm'd.
why do I humble thus my self, and suing
for peace, reap nothing but repulse and hate?
But my anger, my frustration takes me
away from myself. I am forced to speak
with you in front of others – that social
media surveillance, data harvest
the seasonal ritual of leadership
ambition; to rule over those who so
willingly cede their privacy to start-
up glee, to the big picture, to global
marketplace frenzy. What chance did we have,
really, 'at the end of the day', 'when all
is said and done': reduced to characters
counted out as brevity, the abridged
storyline of life. It's so easy
to badmouth me – and in your confinement,
out of the abuse you are suffering,
forget the abuse you meted out… truth
is relative in the swirl of the new
panopticon, which is not to reduce
the scale of your suffering, but to say
suffering happens simultaneously.
None of us can afford to deny
our complicity until agency
is totally denied or lost – I am
saying you still have room to act, to speak
with shared voice, to reach out to those who stand
with you though they risk all in doing so.
Never let the loss of light deny light!
Stand with all condemned, stand with those women
who are forced to say they've equality
when they've none, stand with those who have lost rights
to the power complex that is whiteness,
stand for those whose cultures want space to breathe.
Even chained and crushed by the false 'freedom'

of the 'silicon revolution' — that new
conservatism manipulated
by the same old power desiring –
you have the ability to speak out.
Touch the hand offered, make a bridge across
class and 'race' and property and gender.
No? Then we lose a moment, we lose hope
for reconciliation. Are we lost?

CHOR: To make an antivenin a venom
has to be sourced – we construct the market.

SAM: I want to call myself a feminist
but enjoy the privileges gender forms
have allotted me – such 'secrets' are those
truths I don't want out there in the broader
community... I am selective when
it comes to my rights of 'privacy'? I
don't know. I speak out of imprisonment!

CHOR: *Yet beauty, though injurious, hath strange power,*
after offence returning, to regain
love once possest, nor can be easily
repuls't, without much inward passion felt
and secret sting of amorous remorse.

SAM: The beauty myth cannot be a token
in this catastrophe – my vanity
is formed of doubt and hubris and *desire*.

CHOR: We show clear bias, seek authority,
direct the songs within your story – such

insights allow propositions
to condition propositions;
we set the tables and spread out
gifts and favours – a narrative
deal in which the manner of telling will
determine the reception we aim for.
And so revenge porn shaming, and so ploys
of 'reverse racism', and so the control
of discourse around 'two wrongs don't make a right'
when the wrongs have left nothing for the wronged
to have taken from them – just virtual
possessions bargained in and out of view
like cryptocurrencies. Or the road built
through vestigial bushland so resisted
but a few years later travelled by those
who protested – spilt milk, reality
reprocessed through random access memory
breaking down or made obsolete.
And then we lapse into comparatives –
it was like, a comparison might be
drawn, but it was a different era,
and that sharp reef upon which the empire
is wrecked – CONTEXT! Should we lament?
So many conflicted voices
is it possible to get consensus?
How do we get around 'Women for Trump'?
Why do we need to take them up?
How unpick hidden agendas?
How define art against colonial
statuary – historical
praise of TRIUMPHS?
We fear the loss of the domestic
but deny markers of the despotic?
What is that echo that outruns the text?
Does it make you shudder to hear:
Therefore God's universal Law
gave to the man despotic power

over his female in due awe...?
Research the dynamics,
and take literary scholarship
to the words that prick our ears – and
worry over those shifts and slippages:
most shines and most is acceptable above.
Or has Samson missed the point – lost the hope
of changing course, of making right the wrongs?
But had we best retire, I see a storm?

SAM: *Fair days have oft contracted wind and rain.*

CHOR: *But this another kind of tempest brings.*

SAM: *Be less abstruse, my riddling days are past.*

CHOR: We are being straight forward, making
transition across a plain that shakes with hate,
or rather shakes with hubris. The challenge
of giant to giant for public praise, for self
affirmation. A display for all those
small arms manufacturers who would
break into the bigtime on the back of death.
Even a suburban gunsmith is full
of adrenaline, over-excited
at the prospect of giant taking on giant.
No we're getting down to testosterone:
no *sumptuous Dalila floating this way.*

SAM: You mean like 'arms for peace'? How will this end?

CHOR: No time left to wonder, he's upon us.

HARAPHA: I am not here to commiserate – you've
got what was coming to you – but I wish
I'd had the chance to beat you on the field,
to show the world I am superior.
Harapha is a name like Samson that
should make the earth shake, cutting edge bludgeon
stealth maximum firepower high yield
destructive force pinpoint accuracy
and psychologically devastating.
So, I want to scan your construction, your
design specifications and see how
we compare. Our peoples, our beliefs, our
causes, our devotions, our outrages
driven by witnessing brutality
and wrong, must be pushed aside as we stand
side by side, judged competitively.

SAM: I've lost my thirst for being the hero.

HAR: I take that as misinformation – a taunt
come out of your being broken by mill
and chains, deprived of the sunlight you fed
on – those cascading headlines: Samson breaks
an army with an Ass's Jaw! I would have
tossed your carcass onto the Ass's bones.
But beating you now would be a hollow
victory – I lose because of your state.

SAM: I am drenched in light. Do what you 'have to
do'! But we are brothers of flesh and wire –
we should share space and not drive each other

from it. We could embrace, we could give hope.

HAR: Words twist about our compulsions – I see
your blindness, you see mine. How do we touch
each other when we are programmed not to,
unless it's to eliminate the flesh?

SAM: I have lists of answers – versions of 'me'
I could unload. I have scripts, I have source
code flowing through my spinal column. But
I have lost my resistance to malware
and can't say 'woman is to blame', I can't
say *your* people or *my* people, I can
only say 'people'. But I other 'me',
and having no role to play abandon
hope. You must see that you are trapped inside
their war machine, that *they* feed on heroes.
Go *put on all thy gorgeous arms, thy Helmet
and Brigandine of brass, thy broad Habergeon.
vant-brass and Greves, and Gauntlet, add thy Spear
a Weavers beam, and seven-times-folded shield.*
But I will be as I am. What you see
is what you'll get. Not that the fight has gone
out of me, but my fight will give no
boost to television ratings, no boost
to news junkies who feed on my image.

HAR: *Thou durst not thus disparage glorious arms
which greatest Heroes have in battel worn,
thir ornament and safety, had not spells
and black enchantments, some Magicians Art
arm'd thee or charm'd thee strong* – it's all very
well of you to have your epiphany
but I can see and stand for history

in the making. I trust technology
and ignore your hypocrisy, Samson.

SAM: *I know no Spells, use no forbidden Arts*
but know my old ways weren't the ways of God.
To slaughter is not to answer the wrongs.
Either way. On both sides. Which does not mean
I have found my way through the ghosts of bush
we've destroyed, or deleted the plastics
from the seas – but I am aware of my
own contradiction, the dilemma of
being. My hair, my strength, was cultural.
I wore dreadlocks as resistance to such
status quo. My loss of control was both
inside and outside the machine – rather,
it harnessed anger, alienation,
and confusion. It 'radicalised' for
its own self-serving ends. Maybe our Gods
are hidden behind the propaganda
and would not have us behave as others
tell us they wish? Are we to transfer our
rivalry to God v. God? Is that it?

HAR: It is hard to resist the temptation
to point out that your God has abandoned you
to prison, to slavery, to blindness.
Delivered you into enemy hands!
to paraphrase the propagandist's text.
And then to compare… I am standing here
with my God at my shoulder, while you were
disarmed by the barber! But a guilt stirs,
I'll admit – it's easy to summon God
when one's enemy is covered in dirt.

SAM: All these indignities, for such they are
from thine, these evils I deserve and more,
acknowledge them from God inflicted on me
justly, yet despair not of his final pardon
whose ear is ever open; and his eye
gracious to re-admit the suppliant;
and, against logic, I hope for the same
for you. And in metaphors of stasis
and transport, I have – we have – missed the bus,
this accordance of data and caches
and memory banks. This cloud about us
broken into, dispersed, holding a shared
identity: all our particulars
sharing space but in separate quarters.
Sometimes science has something to show us?

HAR: How does a murderer and robber call
on any God to validate a wrong?

SAM: And you're saying your violence is in some
way more legitimate and spiritual
than mine? Between us, we twist language…

HAR: Again, temptation… who is in control
and who isn't is easily turned to
serve the triumphant. Instead of the land
being shared, the greatest fire
power is presented as being in
the right? Time is to put it to the test?
A definition of existence or
a way to keep the arms industry
in business. Perpetual profit, discord.
Well, I too am just doing a job.

SAM: I married into your society.
I celebrated in your capital.
I have no innate desire for conflict.
I am sexist, I am a bigot, I
have benefited from the praise of my
peers – been privileged above others.
I have unwittingly betrayed others.
I have worshipped myself and used God as
an excuse. But never doubt I have faith,
that I believe in something greater
than the self. The state manipulates all
of us for its own ends – wealth and power
are end results, and if theology
will serve such outcomes then it will threaten
anything that threatens it. I can no
longer trace blame though I know blame is what
I have to cling onto, and it is blame
that will undo me, and undo you, too.
What I am sure about, surrounded by
those enslaved from nations, and from
many peoples, is that wrong is not hard
to distinguish – I don't need my eyesight
for that. Hostile acts against all people.

HAR: I do know the shame each of us will bring
in allowing capital punishment
to take the weight of failed community.

SAM: You say this so easily, but what do
you do about it? Armchair protester,
giant of your privatised morality!
Boaster surveying me in endgame!

HAR: How dare you insult one who is trying –

against his grain – to sympathise with you!
You dishonour me – my integrity!

Sᴀᴍ: I don't trust you, I don't trust anyone –
do you expect a calm and rational
discussion from someone being tortured?

Hᴀʀ: How do enemies find a language
of friendship without stirring worse hatred?

Sᴀᴍ: Yes, I am struggling against my conscience
and against my chains, wanting to tear you
limb from limb. A disturbed pathology.
Leave me! Have some mercy on my torment!

Hᴀʀ: I too am conflicted – I both deplore
and revel in your dire circumstances.

Cʜᴏʀ: *His Giantship is gone somewhat crestfall'n,
stalking with less unconsci'nable strides,
and lower looks, but in a sultrie chafe.*

Sᴀᴍ: *I dread him not, nor all his Giant-brood,
though Fame divulge him Father of five Sons
all of Gigantic size, Goliah chief.*

Cʜᴏʀ: *He will directly to the Lords, I fear,
and with malitious counsel stir them up
some way or other yet further to afflict thee.*

SAM: What, have me killed and end my misery?
I doubt it – I crush more grain, make more flour
than a dozen other slaves. I earn my
keep! And the grist for the mill is fake news-
worthy more than anything else they can
cook up – no photoshopping my demise,
it's there on a platter for them. His acts
of punishment, his jealous connivings
will end my misery. Hate in his hands
will be my deliverance and under-
mine their tools, invasion of privacy.
When our world has reached such degradation
enemies are friends and friends enemies.

CHOR: We are entangled in your fate and death
is death however it comes – we cannot
stand and condone what we have contrived.
In the killing of earth
none of us feel invincible –
the brute and boist'rous force of violent men
hardy and industrious to support
tyrannic power, but raging to pursue
the righteous and all such as honour Truth;
he all thir Ammunition
and feats of War defeats
in saying, Never in my name commit
your acts of violence, Never in my name
fetishise your weapons, never make use
of tradition to defend warfare – it
has no place in homes or schools or public
buildings, nor in the fields nor paddocks
nor in remnant forests or bushland nor
in deserts made by time or enacted
by human intervention. Hear the girl
speak out against gun violence, hear her speak
for her lost classmates, for the everyday

moments of school life – no more… her words ring
through myth and history and across borders
and boundaries… she said NEVER NEVER
NEVER will they again… she said it on
the March of Their Lives, and we must listen
and read and absorb and witness against
what we come from. Shift. Change. Alter. Value
without the desire for a victory
or profit or sceptre.
The mass can shift as much
as the individual. Samson,
death will never be an answer.
But who is this trending this way,
a staff of power in their hand?
By his habit I discern him now
a Public Officer, and now at hand.
his message will be short and voluble.

PUBLICK OFFICER: I have come to direct speech to Samson.

CHOR: *His manacles remark him, there he sits.*

OFF: *Samson, to thee our Lords thus bid me say:*
your strength is legendary and the state
requires a demonstration so it
can validate its greater strength – this is
what states do, I am sure you agree, being
a product of a state we defeated.
With Sacrifices, Triumph, Pomp, and Games
will banner the Facebook page, and such likes
as never accrued before will surely test
the efficiency of where state and private
industry interface – but we accept
such anxiety with exultation!

We'll run you through the filters and have you fit
for our illustrious audience – from
billionaires to movie stars with the odd
winner of a 'meet Sam!' competition!
When it comes to the top end of town we
are all much the same – power knows power.

SAM: I refuse. This is no longer a rites
issue, but one of ratings. I serve earth,
I serve breath, I serve all life and belief.

OFF: Come! You are no floating signifier!

SAM: *Have they not Sword-players, and ev'ry sort*
of Gymnic Artists, Wrestlers, Riders, Runners,
juglers and Dancers, Antics, Mummers, Mimics,
but they must pick me out with shackles tir'd,
and over-labour'd at thir publick Mill,
to make them sport with blind activity?
do they not seek occasion of new quarrels
on my refusal to distress me more,
or make a game of my calamities?
return the way thou cam'st, I will not come.

OFF: They will have little time for semantics!

SAM: The discourse is entwined. We can't take what
is *now* without taking in what has come
before. That's why prejudice jags against
the best efforts to undo wrongs and make
them right. Unless we see the sins that lead
to sin, we can't unpick the wrong. Complex,

as Derrida said… Complex thinking
is often as necessary as our
actions that must follow. I am saying that
it is easy to lapse into a hate
if hate has underwritten history.
Begin by undoing all colonial
interiors, work with sharing the space
we have from history's evil fallout.
If not, we will be stuck, and servitude
will be called equality by those on
top of the pile. No, I will not appear
as a performing clown for anyone!

OFF: Such a reply will cause great displeasure –
even misery can be made much worse.

SAM: Then move fast and let them feel discomfort…

OFF: I am sorry for the consequences.

SAM: Of that I am sure – there's only sorrow.

CHOR: This is likely fuel on the fire, Samson!
What is bad for you now will be made worse.

SAM: My dreadlocks are back and my strength intact –
my transgression has been punished and now
that I am armed and dangerous you suggest
I put on a show, validate the march
advance retire left right? I've done too
many military parades! Should

I desecrate a growing self-knowledge,
this overwhelming light out of darkness?
You play it both ways – urging me on then
suggesting restraint? *Our* absurdity!

CHOR: And yet here you perform for them also,
turning the wheel that feeds them, makes them strong.

SAM: They feed me and I feed them – labour.
The exploited factory worker serving
the wealthier – maybe poor though you
be poorer. The exploiters don't purchase
the products I make, they take their money
and purchase artisan goods, defining
their difference in buying power they have
accrued from exploiting such labour as
mine, the other prisoners, too. Such rip-offs
cut across our ethnic and cultural
differences while devaluing *all* our
identities. *This* is the vision of
strength I have been granted – to disconnect
labour from exploitation, to undo
the ways of all states and all death machines.
I won't perform, I won't go on display!

CHOR: We serve ourselves but wish to serve you, too.

SAM: They may try to drag me to their buildings.
Should I go I go with a purpose that
suits my conscience not design. We make
such choices in macro and micro ways.
With or without enhancements I make *choice*.

CHOR: How will this end? The future is murky.

SAM: *Be of good courage, I begin to feel*
some rouzing motions in me which dispose
to something extraordinary my thoughts.
I with this Messenger will go along,
and try to resolve my contradictions –
respect our law, their law, and natural
law, find a way through prospect and refuge.
If there be aught of presage in the mind,
this day will be remarkable in my life
by some great act, or of my days the last,
but I will not be consumed by vengeance.

CHOR: The human in the cyborg is human –
conscience is the enhancement that matters.

OFF: The captains of industry have spoken –
know their wealth endows universities
and builds huts for people they've dispossessed
just as your captains have dispossessed to give
rewards to those who have stood the test. Where
power is power must be followed or
suffer the consequences! Front up now
or we shall find such Engines to assail
and hamper thee, as thou shalt come of force,
though thou wert firmlier fastn'd then a rock.

SAM: *I could be well content to try thir Art,*
which to no few of them would prove pernicious.
Such methodologies will only result
in the oppression I now feel – they will
crush and they will crush their own spirits in

doing so. The cycles of violence do
loop for-loop perform varying repeat
execution this flow iteration
is a statement imperative breakdown.
I stand by you and stand against us all.
Early exit? Continuation? Hope?

OFF: *I praise thy resolution, doff these links:*
by this compliance thou wilt win the Lords
to favour, and perhaps to set thee free.

SAM: In the words of a woman I now see
more clearly: 'Well, he would say that, wouldn't
he!' This swirl of God and nation and self
and religion, the common good that is
never in common. How do I find my
way through these contradictions, led by one
who amalgamates best interests with 'truth'?

CHOR: Go, and may all peoples
see what you are willing
to do for them – to a general
humanity, to open pathways
to all variations on fair angels
and visions. To link the fate of humans
with the fate of the biosphere, to care
for the animals and plant, for all life.
This is a revolution outside
of violence, but a revolution that
will no doubt be met with bitter response.
The redistribution of strength is not
a carving up of the body, it is
a sharing of tolerance, a sharing
out of property. A redistribution.

But here is old Manoa moving fast
as his legs can carry him! Youthful zest!
Is he hoping to discover his son
and impart good news? Has something shifted?

MAN: The city is erupting with the news
that Samson is on his way to their party –
and though it pains me that they might force him
to do things demeaning I have great hope
that he will be granted his liberty.

CHOR: *That hope would much rejoyce us to partake
with thee; say reverend Sire, we thirst to hear.*

MAN: I have fallen at the knees of a great
captain of industry – one who has sucked
the hills dry of ore, who has thrown baubles
to the people telling them they are
lucky s/he cares so much! That emphatic
common touch, that ol' hail fellow well met!
stuff. I offered a hefty 'donation'
to the political party of choice –
a party which treats outsiders like dirt
but one that will, nonetheless, twist and turn
on matters of 'business'. And one cannot
doubt their commitment 'issues of faith'!
For Samson, they can have my honour, too!

CHOR: Children rely on their guardians while
moving towards an age when they might care
for those less able to manage themselves.
There are reversals and inversions here.

MAN: I will gain from tending him, soothing his
damaged eyes, places where chains have bitten.
I simply cannot believe that it was
part of God's plan to build him up to thrust
him down. My thinking has shifted. So, too,
has my understanding. God is served by
compassion, not by triumphs. It's how we read
a situation that leads to justice.
And since his strength with eye-sight was not lost,
God will restore him eye-sight to his strength.

CHOR: We hope for all our sake. It's so easy
for the group to damage aspiration:
interfere with your self-efficacy.
We join you in hope, in affirmation.

MAN: Yes, I know you are with us in spirit.
But O what a noise! What on earth is that
hideous noise? Horrible… distraught!

CHOR: *Noise call you it or universal groan*
as if the whole inhabitation perish'd,
blood, death, and deathful deeds are in that noise,
ruin, destruction at the utmost point.

MAN: It is the sound of annihilation!
It is the exhaling of death itself!
It is remorseless! Have they killed Samson?

CHOR: O! It's your son doing the slaughtering!

MAN: NO! Never, he would not kill again – those
old ways are not his ways now! His blindness
gave him a vision – an end to bloodshed!
It must be some horrendous accident!
What shall we do, stay here or run and see?

CHOR: *Best keep together here, lest running thither
we unawares run into dangers mouth,*
though it shames us to think like this – surely
a weapon has been triggered while Samson
has been wheeled through the parade, maybe
stumbling on a trigger and his massive
strength a force not reckoned with, outside those
safeguards weapons manufacturers tout
to their followers as inviolable!
And at the moment of ignition sight
comes back to Samson so he knows slaughter?
As if more dead people – more dead children –
will ease the agony of past losses.
Death is death is death. Simple, brutal sum.
An equation beyond the most brilliant
military scientists it would seem. What
is to be done with brute reality?

MAN: I fail here – part of me delights in his
loss of shame through default, and part of me
is ashamed I would revert to hatred.

CHOR: Are we to be caught in a paradox
and let it direct our morality?

MAN: I have no answer being inside this
moment, but I know 'belief' will take us

down paths without second thought. We will hear.

CHOR: *Of good or bad so great, of bad the sooner;*
for evil news rides post, while good news baits.
And now we see a messenger moving
fast towards us – soon we will know the facts.

MESSENGER: The horror! A scene of devastation.
A spectacle I hope I will never
have to behold again – such nightmares will
pursue me – beyond imagination –
and soon the fallout will eat the distance
and affect friend and foe alike, no one
will win from this event, this unleashing!

MAN: *The accident was loud, & here before thee*
with rueful cry, yet what it was we hear not,
no Preface needs, thou seest we long to know.

MESS: *It would burst forth, but I recover breath*
and sense distract, to know well what I utter.

MAN: *Tell us the sum, the circumstance defer.*

MESS: Buildings stand but flesh disintegrated.
This, the 'evolution' of weapons.
Poisoned property where no life exists.

MAN: Were the language of destruction
written out of vocabularies, but it

is not. We hunger for such descriptions
for all the terror they bring close to us.

MESS: Witnessing makes for a life's commitment.

MAN: But Samson was more than flesh!

MESS: Samson lives?

MAN: Is my hope despite ubiquitous death.

MESS: It is pain on pain to tell the father
that his son is destroyed – no matter
that he was part machine and part human,
his humanity was killed when humans
fell about him. His essence has been lost.

MAN: You speak in riddles and it is torture.

MESS: Then said plain and simple, Samson is dead.

MAN: This is agony! I had picked my way
through metaphors of destruction thinking
there'd be a righteous outcome. All moments
of his childhood shared with family flashed
through memory – I knew him gone but willed
his presence. One time when we were passing
a field of burnt stubble he – eagle-eyed –
noticed a wisp of smoke from a burnt log

rising against a hazy sky. Look! he
said, We must let someone know or a strong
wind will incite a new fire with no one
to watch over it. We all laughed and said,
The fire is spent and though it's still hot, dry,
and volatile, there's nothing here for fire
to grip. But he insisted, and fire trucks
were called in. It was discovered the log
was burning hot in its interior
and would have exploded, raining sharp sparks
far beyond its location, and likely
setting the entire district alight.
I was thinking of this as the talk of
death and destruction whirled about, knowing
he was dead, but thinking of him in life.
I like to think of him relishing life,
not caught in death's machine we made of him.

MESS: I should add, that he survived initial
exposure, and seeing what had happened
chose to let the radiation consume...

MAN: him? What are you saying? Yet more riddles!

MESS: He chose to die with those who'd died with him.

MAN: *Self-violence*? No! To die among his foes?

MESS: To have destroyed and be destroyed, all our
fates are intertwined. When there is nothing
left the wrong and right of it are lost.
We make war as we kill earth, our witness.

MAN: Irony grinds us into poisoned dirt.
The satirist who lampoons the problems
without making any change within them-
selves. The eye-witness to our own demise
that abdicates responsibility!

MESS: So I file my report as if affect
is secondary. Without prejudice?
Impossible. And language doesn't work.
The morning Trumpets Festival proclaim'd
through each high street: little I had dispatch't
when all abroad was rumour'd that this day
Samson should be brought forth to shew the people
proof of his mighty strength in feats and games;
I sorrow'd at his captive state, but minded
not to be absent at that spectacle.
The building was a spacious Theatre
half round on two main Pillars vaulted high,
with seats where all the Lords and each degree
of sort, might sit in order to behold,
the other side was op'n, where the throng
on banks and scaffolds under Skie might stand;
I among these aloof obscurely stood
but feeling something was amiss, set up
a camera on a balcony, and took
myself to safe ground. A premonition?
Inside information? Conspiracy?
There's no one left to unpick it other
than you to whom I remain so useful.
I should add, that this event was the end-
game of the military parade,
the icing on the state's cake of glory.
So Samson was brought forth all decked out as
suits displays of conquest, the musicians
revelling in their moment in the sun,
thinking of record sales and those favours

bestowed on them outside usual channels.
Surrounded by citizen soldiery
armed with AR15s, concealed handguns,
missile launchers loaded with tactical
nukes, heavy armour with nerve gas filled shells.
A bonanza from world's weapons bazaars!
Viz, a strongly cross-cultural array
of death-making – human innovation!
So, unseeing but aware of the fire-
power surrounding him, Samson put
on a display of raw strength that staggered
onlookers – the crowd fell still then raised its
arms in wonder, almost worship. It feared
but grew addicted. Then to mark a break
on the action, his keepers positioned
him between the pillars of the venue,
and suddenly seeing where he really
was and who he really was and what lay
before him, he spoke out, Now you captains
of industry, you have seen what I can
do, and you think my strength is at your
beck and call, an extension of your tools
of control. You think I serve your worldview
well. But think again, because though I have
resolved to leave my life of violence, you
have short-circuited my self-control. The
violence within me will act of its own
volition – self-fulfilling prophecy.
I see myself doing what I am
about to do and cannot prevent
it happening. These pillars forced aside
will bring your world crashing down upon you.
And then everyone but Samson died, who
seeing his destruction gave up his will
for life. But this is metaphor, as said,
not a skerrick of property was harmed –
all were dead though such an accident had

been well and truly planned for. As you'd know,
each weapon has multiple fail-safes, who
would have thought that they all could fail like that?
My camera kept recording. I escaped.
For now. I am here before you. Waiting.

CHOR: We are inside false news and call it truth.
The 'truth' that is liked the most is the truth
we will manage the future by – those funds
of knowledge adjusted for inflation.
In the market place the devices of
our communication will find safety,
protection, a receptive community.

SEMICHORUS: It's universal this head in the sand
while governments and industry exploit
people's struggle to get on with life.
Using taxation and the hook of jobs
to make devices that maim and kill while
calling it liberty, an extension
of personal freedom they don't really
have. Who wouldn't rather sit back and watch
Game of Thrones as a culturally apt
equivalent in terms of turning off
from reality. Participation
is sold as a hashtag on devices
that extract the heart of country, delete
villages and belief, swap the local
for the global. The same world that allowed
allows genocide to undo frameworks
of humanity, allows systemic
killing to thrive in primetime, and also
off-Broadway. In Australia fame is made
on land stolen and still the stolen kids
see stealing of a new generation

discussed on that same primetime TV – no
shift in the world addicted to sport as
diversion, to making more than we work.

SEMICHOR: Samson saw this in his blindness but could
not escape the reach of 'intelligence'
services, the shadowy world, dark web.
The cloud is milked for information we
so readily offer for surveillance.
Birds of the spirit are shot down in droves.
The flora and fauna of disputed
land will suffer, also. Poets don't share
language for fear of letting go
of their hold on what they possess – let them
know that a poet by design can have
nothing beyond speaking. That once spoken
it is gone. A poet can own nothing.
Fame is delusion, fame is destruction.
Let go. Let go. Let go.

MAN: The script says that I should now console you
all – say, 'No time for lamentation now…
That Samson died heroically, bringing
death to the enemy. But the problem
is that we are enemies to ourselves,
that we are enemy to life outside
our own, and so often to our own lives.
The story moves on from his wife, who we
might presume has been lost in the slaughter.
Should we not think of her further, should her
inherited constraints, the marketing
of family and property, the sell
of ideology as defence of
justice when it serves those who wield its tools,
in copious Legend, or sweet Lyric Song?

Not much is left of the original
textuality – it fades through time and
politics, but does the ethics of all
being equal under the melanoma
sun shift? Is life some trick of language?
Study the colours of feathers without
interfering with the parrot, the light.

CHOR: If you are looking for resolution,
if you are hoping for a catharsis,
then look elsewhere. But we advise you to
be quick about it, because threnody
is between the notes of the sweetest pop
lyric, and all the entertainment out
there won't stop the machine making holes for
you to fall through. But then, we feed it, don't
we? So easy to go home and pretend
opinion is a projection of your
inner strength. That we want what's best for ALL.

THE END

Fit and Few Samson
Tim Cribb

After the war in Heaven, returning to earth in Book VII of *Paradise Lost*, Milton, now half-way through his epic, prays for guidance. He prays to his muse, but not to the muse of epic poetry, Calliope, nor even to Polyhymnia, veiled muse of sacred poetry, but to Urania, muse of astronomy, the science of the heavens. But it is not literally to her that he speaks. His prayer is addressed to 'the meaning, not the name' for, rightly understood, pagan myths are figurings of Hebraic and Christian revelations. Thus interpreted, the Urania who, he says, 'Visitst my slumbers Nightly' and whose promptings then continue to guide the labour of composition 'when Morn / Purples the East,' this Urania can only be a figure for the Holy Spirit: she must come from God, and, since God cannot be compelled, the inspiration therefore comes when he is asleep, unconscious. Interpreted by the book of neuroscience, this will be during the REM phase of brain activity, when, without conscious volition, problems are solved and creative connections forged. Interpreted by the Protestant Bible, Urania's visitations are an act of grace, amazing grace, and, since they come in answer to prayer, a sure sign that he who prayed must be, from moment to moment, in a state of grace. Therefore Milton can sing on, his 'mortal voice unchang'd', the same voice as before he 'fell on evil dayes' and despite now being 'with dangers compast round'.

In what he called 'the cool element' of prose, Milton's mortal voice had been heard across Europe for twenty years, for example in tracts defending the execution of the King or justifying the massacre of Irish Catholics. Heads of state had heard from him writing to them as Secretary for the Foreign Tongues in the name of the Council or of Lord Protector Cromwell. He had written, for example, to the young Louis XIV and Cardinal Mazarin, asking them to lend asylum to Protestant refugees fleeing from

Piedmont, where the Duke of Savoy was cleansing his land of heretics. On that urgent occasion, Milton had risen above the cool element, gathered his singing robes about him and spoken directly to God in the poem-prayer: 'Avenge O Lord thy slaughtered saints, whose bones / Lie scattered on the Alpine mountains cold'. Verse or prose, it is the same impulse behind the voice, in the thick of Europe's wars of religion. But that was then. Now, the son of the King Milton had voted to execute had been restored to his father's throne, Milton's tracts had been burned by the public hangman, and he himself had been imprisoned. That so vocal and militant a regicide was then spared execution and allowed to retreat to the obscurity of a country village is astonishing. Others were not so lucky.

Though spared, Milton now had to live with the fact that the new Jerusalem on earth had not come to pass and the people of England had proved unworthy of their high calling. The Restoration was even popular. This meant that, though spared by the State, he might yet fall victim to the mob – hence at the end of his prayer to Urania he sombrely reflects that the pagan muse, Calliope, could not save her poet, Orpheus, when he was torn apart by the drunken women Bacchantes. Nonetheless, though the people were changeable and had proved unworthy, his voice would not change. Yet, after being at the height of Europe's Renaissance culture and at the centre of its politics as a leading figure in the first modern revolution, he now finds himself writing something that, in Chapter Three of *Kafka: Toward a Minor Literature*, Deleuze and Guattari call "minority literature". "Minority" here is an eccentric, deliberately politicized re-definition of "minor" to designate not a quantitative relation but 'the revolutionary conditions for every literature within the heart of what is called "great" (or established) literature'. All that he can ask of Urania now is that she assist his voice to find those few still fit to hear it.

Small wonder, then, that when Milton introduces *Samson Agonistes* with an essay on tragedy he remarks that 'this work never was intended for the stage'. Nor would the licensed stages of the Theatres Royal at Covent Garden, Drury Lane and the Haymarket have accepted it. So this Christian tragedy remained un-staged in England for over two hundred years. It took another 'man with a vision', someone with 'an unshakable inner conviction' that enabled him to 'walk through all his life holding fixed before his inward eye something that no one else saw quite as he did,' someone with 'the absurdity of a saint'. That is how Robert Speaght describes William Poel in his biography of the founder of the Elizabethan Stage Society, who first put *Samson Agonistes* on the stage – though not on the popular stage, now constrained by the licence of commercial profit. He presented it in the lecture theatre of the Victoria and Albert Museum in April 1900. The audience, initially respectably numerous, gradually dwindled as the performance proceeded, so those few staying to the end were presumably fit. Indeed, the critic of *The Morning Post* recorded that 'There were a few' for whom 'it was as though they had listened to a... Burial Service... performed... over a stranger that was yet themselves' – a fascinating insight into an unexpected frisson of the uncanny. Eight years later came the tercentenary of Milton's birth, so in December 1908 Poel revived his production and took it to the New Theatre in Cambridge, following on from the newly formed Marlowe Society's production of *Comus* in the same theatre, directed by Rupert Brooke, both productions under the aegis of Milton's old college, Christ's. It was Christ's College again, together with the continuing Marlowe Society and the late Robin Callan of Grantchester, who commissioned John Kinsella's re-working of *Comus* for Milton's quatercentenary in 2008.

Now we come to Kinsella's latest dialogue with Milton, *Samson Agonistes*. Since it is anticipated at the time of writing that this will receive a stage production in Australia and a studio or radio production by the Marlowe Society in Cambridge, let us put some questions to the two texts of the kind that actors and directors necessarily have to ask when making choices about how actual bodies should move and speak on a stage.

First, where are the characters, in what place? Milton's published text first lists 'The Persons' in the play and there are six, plus the Chorus. It then sets the place: 'The scene before the Prison in Gaza'. Milton is thinking of a theatre that no longer existed, the Ancient Greek theatre, so he probably envisaged a broad but shallow raised acting area for the principals, backed along its length by a wall with a central door, all standing above a much deeper acting area for the Chorus. It is onto the raised acting area that Samson enters through the door, which thereby becomes localised as the prison gate. However, all this revivalist apparatus is swept away by his first words:

> A little onward lend thy guiding hand
> To these dark steps, a little furder on.

To whom is he speaking? One expects a boy or servant or some such to lead him and one is in fact mentioned in the Biblical source. But there is no Boy in the list of Persons, nor does the text supply words for any such character. This lacuna, this absence and silence opens a void which immensely amplifies the words actually uttered. They take on the resonance of prayer. Even were a physical guide to be supplied on stage, Samson speaks past him or her to an invisible addressee, so that what might seem like a simple practical request becomes an appeal for help in summoning the strength to take the last few steps to reach an ultimate goal. Place becomes merely incidental; it is swallowed up in numinous space, the space defined by Erich Auerbach in the first chapter of his great *Mimesis*, where he contrasts the daylight practicality and presentness of Homer's telling of the return of Odysseus with the dark mystery and suspense of the story of Abraham and Isaac in Genesis, where God 'enters the scene from some unknown height or depth and calls'. Our word "theatre" comes from the Greek verb "theaesthai", to see, and the Greek theatre was a place to see a show and where the gods did appear. The main actor in *Samson Agonistes* can never be shown and what we see on stage is not merely a blind man but the blindness of Man. For all the neoclassical apparatus, Milton's imagination is, as Jebb observed a century ago, profoundly Hebraic.

The location of Kinsella's text is also undefinable, but not in the same way. His text is dedicated, it is an offering, but the offering is not to a god, with the implied gesture of arms lifted to the heavens or the rising smoke of sacrifice. It is 'for Israel and Palestine', both comparable to gods in their power to impel their peoples with the identities and passions of nationalism, but they are on a level with each other and the writer. We are no longer in the vertically oriented, God-haunted space of *Genesis* but in the horizontally oriented, political space of current affairs. Since the text is offered to Palestine and Israel we assume that "the" prison in Gaza must be the main prison. Do we perhaps know about this prison? Have we seen it on TV or in a newspaper? Is Samson in effect an Israeli secret weapon captured by the Palestinians? Followed through, these surmises lead to clearly untenable conclusions, but that's not so clear during real performance time in a theatre or in the moment of reading. Cued by words such as "Palestine" or "Gaza", our minds cannot but scan the incoming information to see if it matches what we already know from previous experience. Hence such surmises are fleetingly, even unconsciously, entertained before they are ruled out, and even then only provisionally. The result is that the scene is and is not *the* prison in Gaza. It is a prison in a minority literature in the fullest sense of Deleuze and Guattari's special definition of the word: it is deterritorialized.

A moment later, the text tells us the setting is not even the Middle East, for 'the grove of remnant vegetation' where Samson seeks relief is of gumtrees and eucalyptus, which belong in Australia. So now we find ourselves in an extreme grove of the ironized pastoral that is John

Kinsella's distinctive landscape, and there is no relief under the shadow of this red rock. It is the blasted landscape of human geography, scored by migrations and colonisations, scoured by ethnic cleansings, pogroms and genocides. Nor is there anywhere beyond the horizon, no New World, no Eldorado, as there was in Milton's time. We have been round the world many times since then and now meet only ourselves coming back. Still less is there any expectation in this text of the apocalyptic descent from above of a new Jerusalem. So it is not so much that Samson can be in two places at once as that "place" in a globalized world is not what it was. Every time we watch the news we visit several different places, virtually present in rapid succession, and again, in a different way, when we communicate with people on the pocket screens of "social" media, even when not knowing where they are – such activities inevitably condition how we think "place".

Nor can Samson be what he was, which brings us to the other practical question an actor has to answer when preparing to play him: who is he? Milton takes his Samson from the *Book of Judges*. It had been in his mind as a quarry for tragedies since he made a list of possible topics in the Cambridge Manuscript (usually dated to the 1640s), for *Judges* recounts the repeated failure of God's chosen people, whether because of the sins of the government or of the people themselves, to organise society in a way to make it fit for God's purpose. There are also successes. Milton notes that the story of Gideon twice meets his criteria for a Christian play. First there is his smashing of the altars of Baal, a successful iconoclasm, and as such high on the Protestant scale of feats of virtue, and second there is his surprise victory over the Midianites with only a hundred men, achieved by having them hide their torches in pitchers while surrounding the Midianite camp at night, then all together breaking the pitchers so that the sudden blaze gives the impression of a mighty host. As the Geneva Bible explains in a marginal comment: 'These weake menes God used to signifie that the whole victorie came of him'; that is the point.

Similarly, Samson features in the list for his feat in routing the Philistines with only the weak means of the jawbone of an ass for weapon, thereby making clear that the victory can only be attributed to God. Intriguingly, Milton adds to these impeccably Christian criteria two pagan attributes: 'Pyrsophorus, or Hybristes'. The "phorus" part of the first word is from "phorein": to carry, and means he is a bearer, like the chorus of captured women slaves in the *Choephori* of Aeschylus, who enter bearing the "choes" or vessels of libation to be poured for the dead. Samson carries fire. Milton combines this with "sophos", meaning philosophic wisdom, and also prudence, skill in art, even craftiness, and this suggests an ingenious Samson, like Gideon. We think of him only in terms of his exceptional strength, but he was also a wise ruler, for we are twice told in the Bible that he was a judge who ruled Israel for twenty years (*Judges* XV 20, XVI 31). He is one of the success stories in the political history of that time. More importantly, he is later a story of apparent abjection and disaster that is then miraculously changed into victory, and that, together with his Sophos, is his significance for Milton, for his own Muse, Urania, is sister to Sophia, 'eternal wisdom'; they converse together.

What enabled Samson to make wise decisions in government was the same as what enabled him to accomplish his feats of strength and Milton to write his poems: it was because on each occasion he was visited by the Spirit of the Lord. As the King James Bible says before the episode with the jawbone, 'And the Spirit of the Lord began to move him', which the Geneva Bible translates as 'And the Spirit of the Lord began to strengthen him'. And this also explains why Samson is a fire-bearer, for the Spirit itself is a kind of fire and he is associated with fire from the beginning. When the Spirit of God visits his parents in angelic form with the message that they will have a son who has been chosen by God for a special mission, they offer up a sacrifice to give thanks and the angel returns to Heaven in the flame of the sacrifice as if in a column or chariot of fire. When Samson recalls snapping the cords with which his first wife tried to bind him, those 'cords to me were threds / Toucht with the flame' – and flame here is not a metaphor. At the end, 'His fierie vertue' rouses 'From under ashes into sudden flame' and he renews himself like the Phoenix.

It is by the strength of this flame of the Spirit that Samson is a Christian hero. He thereby subsumes the pagan heroes who foreshadow him, especially Hercules, traditionally interpreted as a "figuring" of Samson and mentioned by Milton in his *First Defence of a Christian People* as 'the grand slayer of Tyrants'. He also subsumes all chivalric Romance, all Humanist re-definitions of true nobility, all Renaissance celebrations of fame and glory. As God's champion he is the climax and consummation of all the conquering heroes who have preceded him on the English stage, from Tamburlaine's ambition for 'the sweet fruition of an earthly crown' to Henry V's victory at Agincourt. The difference between him and them is that Samson has been 'solemnly elected' even before birth by God himself 'for some great work' and the glory will therefore be God's. This, as the Chorus says, singles him out from the common herd. The editors of the Longman edition seem somewhat puzzled when they note 'a remarkable series of echoes of Shakespeare's Coriolanus' in the Messenger's speech. But the intertextuality is apt enough, for Coriolanus is the most uncompromising, extreme and absolute of all Shakespeare's heroes. Because Samson is elect, because he is moved by God's Spirit, he not only rises above the common rout but is invested with the impelling power that is driving the times, that Renaissance drive towards absolutism, whether in the arts, as in the building of St. Peter's, or in the theory and practice of monarchy and imperialism, or in revolution and the building of the new Jerusalem. It is the drive evoked by an appalled and fascinated Brecht in section 33 of his 'Short Organum for the Theatre':

Shakespeare's great solitary figures, bearing on their breast the star of their fate, carry through with irresistible force their futile and deadly outbursts; they prepare their own downfall; life, not death, becomes obscene as they collapse; the catastrophe is beyond criticism. Human sacrifices all round.

Brecht had *Hamlet* in mind but his description fits the catastrophe of *Samson Agonistes* even better.

Milton requisitions this heroic dynamism for Samson and does so aware of the problematics involved. It is not that he is troubled by the slaughter of the Philistine elite any more than by Cromwell's slaughter of Roman Catholics (though, departing from the Biblical text, he does make sure the ignorant vulgar escape). What is problematic is precisely his most famous exploit, the pulling down of the temple on his own head as well as on the Philistines, for how can this be distinguished from suicide, the irrevocable crime against the Holy Ghost? And yet the power to accomplish the feat comes from that very inspiration.

Hence Milton's second title for Samson in his exploratory notes comparing Biblical with Classical tragedies: Samson 'Hybristes', meaning excessive. Is he like Achilles, who, in his mistreatment of Hector's body in the *Iliad*, was intoxicated by his own invincibility, or Ajax in his rage slaughtering sheep as dramatized by Sophocles? The verb from which the epithet derives means to run wanton, like an over-fed horse, in Latin translated as "lascivere", which means to be sportive, but to excess. Samson's martial strength and weakness thus turns out to be subtly linked to his sexual strength and weakness, the one begets the other:

> Full of divine instinct ...
> Fearless of danger, like a petty god
> I walked about admired of all...
> Then swoll'n with pride into the snare I fell
> Of fair fallacious looks, venereal trains.

The linkage is indeed problematic in the context of the Protestant Reformation, because in both the martial and the venereal cases what has moved him has been in the first a 'divine instinct', in the second 'an intimate impulse'. Both seemed to come from God, but the second led him into his marriage to the woman of Timna, who betrayed him, and then into his marriage to Dalila, who also betrayed him. How can we know that the one that prompts him to pull down the temple on his own head comes from God, rather than from his own despair? According to the OED, it is during Milton's times that the very word "impulse" hovers between 'A strong suggestion supposed to come from a good or evil spirit' and the modern meaning of 'an application of sudden force causing motion', which of course derives from the mechanics and physics of the new sciences then emerging under the eyes of Urania.

Milton dramatizes in Samson what had troubled the mind of Protestant Europe ever since Luther, in an agony of guilt, found that he could not save his soul by performing the rituals of religion; it was only when the Spirit of God visited him inwardly with assurance of forgiveness that he felt himself to be saved. Calvin turned the screw on this already tense psychology by arguing that, since God was not only just but omniscient, He must already know the fate of those who were to be damned and those who were to be saved. Religion thus became an internal, intensely psychologised and thereby outwardly invisible, inscrutable event. No one can read another's mind, or God's, and this was not only an arcane concern of theology but sometimes of urgent political consequence. For example, Cromwell, outside Edinburgh on 30 August 1650, replies to the General Assembly of the Kirk, whose army he faces, and who have written to explain their decision to support the King: 'Is it therefore infallibly agreeable to the Word of God, all that you say? I beseech you, in the bowels of Christ, think it possible you may be mistaken'. The Elders of the Kirk have of course chosen the opposite side by the same lights as

Cromwell himself.

Milton chooses Samson for hero precisely because, like a contemporary Calvinist, he was chosen by God, and because that is where the problematics reside. It is his own case as a poet. How does a man, especially if he knows himself to be a chosen one, tell the difference between the various impulses to action within him? How can he be sure that a particular impulse comes from God? That is the issue in *Samson Agonistes*. Until the final catastrophe, which is off-stage, the action of the drama is articulated entirely through arguments, appeals and debates, a drama of the mind, conscience-bound to attend to the possibilities of doubts and opposing arguments. Its parallel in actual politics was the New Model Army's great two-week-long debate during the winter of 1647 in St. Mary's Church, Putney about how they, ordinary men, volunteer soldiers, should govern themselves and the country, a debate of world-historical significance that has never found its Thucydides or Hegel. Samson is heroic because he fights an agon of doubt. His self-examination and scruples convert a revenge play into a Christian tragedy whose final carnage can be offered to the glory of God. As well as being the Coriolanus of Renaissance absolutism, Samson is also the Hamlet of Calvinism.

Though framed in very different terms, a similar problematics of free will and moral integrity in a context of violence drives the action of John Kinsella's re-imagining of Samson. Hence the large number of passages from Milton's dramatic poem that Kinsella has no difficulty in incorporating verbatim into his own, such as this:

> O that torment should not be confin'd
> To the bodies wounds…
> But must secret passage find
> To th'inmost mind.

However, this is not the same mind, not the same Samson. To return to the practical questions that actors have to answer: who is this Samson? Milton's hero was one of those few chosen by God 'for some great work', singled out from 'the common rout', like Calvin's elect. Kinsella's Samson *is* that rout, for he is what anthropologists call a "culture hero", a representative figure of the motives, practices and fantasies that constitute a society. He steps straight out of Superhero movies, Marvel comics and (boy) children's toys. His superhuman strength is because he has been enhanced, he is a cyborg, a hero of technology. As such, he is not begotten directly by the Renaissance and Reformation but by the material application of the principles unleashed by those movements in the next major convulsion of the Western world, the Industrial Revolution What distinguishes the Industrial Revolution from one-off political revolutions is that, as Marx and Engels first pointed out in 1848, it is a permanent revolution, continually replacing old products with new ones, together with the productive processes, work practices, social institutions, tastes and desires needed to enable, regulate and consume what is produced. The force driving this perpetual revolution is market competition, and technology, as its handmaid, is thus harnessed to an aggressive dynamic.

If Faust is the signature myth for the Renaissance then the myth for the Industrial Revolution and its applied science is "Frankenstein" (meaning both Victor Frankenstein and his Creature). He enters the arts of the twentieth century through the Futurists and Vorticists and continues, for example, in the half-human, half-robot sculptures of Paolozzi, such as his great 'Homage to Newton', seated in the forecourt of the British Library and modelled on the high-tech architect Richard Rogers.

The original Samson's strength was superhuman but organic; it was in his natural body, in his hair. Kinsella's Samson is no longer a natural body, and that is what makes him representative, as he says:

… I am a child of them all, of
All people who fuse with technology.

That's us. From the amalgams in our teeth, to the titanium screws and plates that mend our bones, to the pacemakers regulating our heart-beats, to the non-mechanical interventions in our biology, such as the aspirin or Viagra in our bloodstreams, or the appetitive pathways laid down in our brains by merchandising corporations, we are prosthetically, chemically and microelectronically modified, whether by enhancement or repair. When these interventions and enhancements are medical we of course embrace them, and we are eager or anxious to embrace the cybernetic in other ways too. One way is by learning how to work with and hence teach our bodies how to behave like machines. We play video games, our hands cradle cellphones, our fingers learn to Twitter, our whole bodies learn to drive. More insidiously, even without actual physical modifications to ourselves, we align ourselves with the world of the cyborg when we go shopping. We then enter the market created by the Industrial Revolution and its competitive dynamics. Responding to its impulsions, we seek out, prefer and choose the most recent, efficient and advanced products we can afford. If we can't afford the latest and best, we hope that, as we look ahead along our time-line, we will be able to do so later, according to our means and according to our versions of the future, whether that be when payday comes round on Friday or when investments mature and the mortgage is paid off. Shopping becomes one of the ways in which we give time itself a structure and meaning, and time in the market of competition continually accelerates. Hence we not only incorporate some of the products and devices we buy into our bodies; we become cyborgs in our minds, for the mental act of choosing, election, means we not only buy the product but buy into the system that produced it; election is interpellation. This is normally by an act of unconscious assent, becoming conscious only on exceptional occasions, such as in a campaign to boycott the products of some controversial national or commercial producer.

Here, then, is 'the secret passage... to th'inmost mind' of Kinsella's *Samson* and why we find installed there a dilemma about choice, free will and purity of motive that resembles the Protestant anxiety about the sources of inspiration. Samson's long hair in Kinsella's version is because he has kept it from the time when he was 'a child of the 60s', with its implications of peace, love and dropping out of conformist society. This is almost the opposite of its meaning in the original myth, replacing physical strength and ability to inflict violence with moral strength to refuse violence. The value of betraying the secret of his strength to Dalila is similarly reversed into 'deep liberty', a refusal of patriarchal dominance. In America, during the Vietnam War, some children of the 60s wedded to those ideals did indeed manage to dodge the draft, and maybe Samson was one of them; yet now he finds himself fighting in and as a war machine. Similarly, both the younger Bush and Clinton evaded the draft, but later, as Presidents and Commanders in Chief, waged wars. How can this be? The point is not the turpitude of individuals but the more far-reaching and troubling one that though Samson might have escaped that particular war this does not mean that he has escaped war, either then or now. That is the fix in which he finds himself.

The challenge for Milton's *Samson* was to distinguish, as he looked into his mind, between those of his impulses, such as sexual attraction or violent aggression, which were fallacious, and those which came authentically from God; the difficulty was that the incarnational God of Protestant Christianity spoke to him through those very same human impulses. This is where Kinsella's use of the Marvel comic superhero comes to bear, for that genre delivers the character of Samson ready-made as culture hero, by definition socially determined. Hence, when Kinsella's Samson looks into his mind, all he can find there is his own social formation. The voice of God has fallen silent, for the position of ultimate source of creation, power, meaning and values He once occupied has been taken over by society. Accordingly, the systematic theology derived from the Bible in which Milton formulated his guiding principles is replaced by sociology, and the founder of that science of humanity is Durkheim. In his 'Conclusion' to *The Elementary Forms of Religious Life* in 1912, Durkheim is quite explicit about the take-over: 'A society has all that is necessary to arouse the sensation of the divine in minds, merely by the power it has over them'. The power can be exerted by external imposition in a coercive way, whether by mob or state violence, or prescriptively through the law. However, because society is composed of individuals, 'this force must also penetrate us and organize itself within us' and is hence mostly consensual and exerted internally. This makes the power of society all the more comprehensive. According to Durkheim, even the categories of space and time and logic, the very means with which we think, do not originate in the mind itself, as Kant had argued, but from our experience of social forms and organization: 'Impersonal reason is only another name for collective thought'. Hence *Suicide* (1897), Durkheim's first major study of his own society, seeks to demonstrate that what people assume to be a highly individual choice is in fact imbued with social necessity. On these terms of analysis, Samson's prison is indeed deterritorialized, for it is his own mind, and he shares it with his enemies.

The problem inherent in this elevation of the social to the category of categories is its tendency towards equivocation of terms and circularity of logic. The descriptive terms to characterise a particular society at a particular moment in time, necessarily taken from that society, are abstracted and projected back onto it in a way that changes their meaning: adjectival attributes are converted into nounal substantives, the contingent solidifies into the structural, snapshots of the diachronic are frozen into evidence of the synchronic. Making society into final source of meaning is nonetheless a very effective means of understanding human behaviour for, if the supernatural is ruled out, how else do we explain ourselves? It thus permeates thinking in social and political sciences and cultural studies, for example in Althusser's theory of interpellation (already resorted to above), or Bourdieu's analysis of the processes of social reproduction, or Foucault's accounts of historical cultures in terms of their prevailing discourses, or Said's application of that idea in the context of imperial control. What these various approaches have in common is that they draw their terms from the situation they are describing and then make those terms into the limiting horizon of that situation's possibilities.

There is thus a formal resemblance between the logic of these human sciences and the principle of the feed-back loop in control engineering, by which systems are designed to be responsive to their own behaviour in such a way as to eliminate deviations from whatever norm defines the system and its function. The new Bible that expanded that particular applied science of engineering into a wider field by combining it with information theory was Norbert Wiener's *Cybernetics: Or Control and Communication in the Animal and the Machine* (1948). Wiener implicitly acknowledges the continuity of cybernetics with the Industrial Revolution when he salutes Clerk Maxwell's paper on governors, delivered to the Royal Society in March 1868, as the first significant contribution to the field of feed-back mechanisms. That is because the centrifugal governor for which Clerk Maxwell provided the mathematical equations was the one that his compatriot, James Watt, had first applied to the steam engine of his partner in business, Robert Boulton, in 1788. Wiener might also have mentioned another paper anticipating his own, presented to the Royal Society by Charles Darwin on behalf of Alfred Russel Wallace in 1858, in which Wallace applies the idea of feed-back mechanisms to animals as well as machines, again with explicit reference to Watt's Governor.

In principle, feed-back mechanisms are homeostatic, that is, they keep things the same, but what they keep the same is typically an overall dynamic system: Watt's Governor enabled Boulton's steam-engine to keep going and keep going faster. The same applies to the social feed-back loop Samson feels installed within himself, in his 'weaponised self', and in the case of a society driven by market competition the experience of the last two hundred years is that it keeps going faster. This drive is what over-rides the young Samson of the Sixties. Norbert Wiener suffered the same experience. Despite his personally peaceful values and inclinations, he found himself voluntarily applying mathematics to the design of control systems to eliminate deviations from the target trajectory in bomb and artillery aiming mechanisms in the Second World War. Appalled, like Robert Oppenheimer, by Hiroshima, he too might well have said, 'I am become Death, the destroyer of worlds'.

Samson can say the same. Made in the image of his society, all he can do is reproduce its dynamics, and these drive towards destruction. Hence the Calvinist language of predestination is co-opted and harnessed to a social mechanism.

> I – preordained, predestined, constructed,
> roll off the A1 production line –
> evil and good and trending and hashtagged.
> I – no petition can save me
> from what they – you all! – have manufactured.

The issue for Milton was: did Samson commit suicide, or was he inspired by God? If the former, he was damned. The issue for Kinsella is: does Samson commit an act of violence? If so, not only does he thereby forfeit his own humanity but he re-enforces an ever-accelerating feed-back loop of violence to which his society condemns itself. In both cases, the dramatists resort to dramaturgical devices to remove the issue from direct presentation so as thereby to entail the audience in the process of self-reflection.

Milton uses the classical convention of stichomythia, a rapid exchange of question and answer, marking the entrance of a new character, especially a Messenger. This makes the exchange seem more like a challenging game of riddles than straightforward information. The convention of the Messenger speech itself arises from the further convention that no physical actions are actually shown on stage. Deprived of the evidence of experience, we cannot vouch for the truth of what is reported. Moreover, in this particular case the Messenger himself can only speculate on what it was that he reports. He says that once Samson had been positioned between the pillars:

> With head a while enclin'd
> And eyes fast fixt he stood, as one who prayd,
> Or some great matter in his mind revolv'd.

"As"? "Or"? This is the great issue of the drama and he cannot tell us which it is! We have been set at an even further metatheatrical remove than when Hamlet, played by an actor, says he has 'that within which passeth show'. The Messenger is reporting what happened in a theatre to an on-stage audience in another theatre and leaves what he saw open to interpretation and no deus ex machina appears to tell us what we should think. The intense privacy of the Protestant moment of communion with God remains inviolate, inscrutable. That Samson was indeed praying, and that God answered his prayer, can only be inferred from the event of the massacre, and a Philistine will have a different interpretation of that history.

Kinsella's *Samson Agonistes* similarly sets the terms defining the issue spinning around themselves and similarly employs a metatheatrical dramaturgy. Samson is, as superhero of society, his own deus ex machina, reflecting back on itself the audience he is reported as addressing. It is the long-haired Samson of the Sixties who speaks, but powerless to break the feed-back loop of the Terminator he has become:

> though I have
> resolved to leave the life of violence, you

have short-circuited my self-control. The
violence within me will act of its own
volition.

The word "cybernetics" is formed from the Greek word for a steersman, "kybernetes"; Samson, like a modern missile, is now on automatic pilot.

Faithful to his source and, as a Humanistically trained poet, amplifying it, Milton dwells on the moment of the catastrophe. Samson shakes and tugs the pillars to and fro 'As with the force of winds and waters pent / When Mountains tremble' until the Philistines are finally crushed to death by the falling masonry; the climax is eruptive, convulsive, sensational. The aftermath, 'all passion spent', consequently feels post-orgasmic. Human feelings have been vectors for the message that God's purpose has been fulfilled. The emphasis on the sensational continues after Samson's death when his father, Manoa, takes control, organizes a party to find the body, 'Soakt in his enemies blood', cleanse it from this pollution, then carry it to 'his Fathers house', where a monument will be built, hung with texts celebrating the hero's deeds 'In copious Legend or sweet Lyric Song'. Milton's text is de facto one of these and thereby closes the circuit of social reproduction.

In Kinsella's text, by contrast, if there is a "villain" in the cast of characters it is Manoa, the voice of patriarchy, and as such the person mainly responsible for inculcating his son with patriarchal values. The text therefore does not give him the last word, nor does it identify with its own story, nor is the ending sensational. It is apocalyptic, in the root sense of uncovering things, especially, since the Biblical *Book of Revelation*, uncovering last things. What it uncovers are precisely the circuits of social reproduction that are bound to lead to the ending. The ending itself is eerily and desolately empty of sensation. Samson appears to have triggered an advanced radiation weapon, either in himself or in the equipment of the accompanying military parade – it may even have been an accident – and the effect of the weapon is to destroy human life but without damaging anything else. All the buildings are left standing, like a surrealist city painted by Chirico. Their property is preserved but the proprietors who commissioned the weapon to protect their property have made themselves extinct. The only "objective" record of the event must be the automatic camera the Messenger set up on a balcony, but he left that behind when escaping. Instead of climax we have irony. The last things begin to be revealed but we will not be there to witness them, for the invisible destruction is still spreading:

> And soon the fallout will eat the distance
> and affect friend and foe alike, no one
> will win from this event, this unleashing!

Cromwell himself participated in the New Model Army's great Putney debate on democracy. Milton was not a participant, but he fervently believed in the Army's mission: to build the new Jerusalem, here and now. He therefore, as Secretary for the Foreign Tongues, made himself ambassador for the cause. It was a mission that professed peace but that nonetheless, on encountering opposition, whether from pagans or Catholics, would declare war, whether in Ireland or Europe or the Caribbean. We now live in a world where the energies of religious belief again flow along the circuits of social and political reproduction and where an actual Jerusalem is now a national capital and hence inevitably drawn into those circuits. I end with a recent poem-fragment by John Kinsella:

> Jerusalem is all, and yet exclusion
> is the call at the walls of endgame.
> Dance of the timekeepers & death.
> A white breath from the New World
> flights bullets in a tableaux of the Old.
> Such diplomacy will pave the way
> with corpses, the embassy of pain.

Biographical Notes

JOHN KINSELLA'S most recent volumes of poetry are *Drowning in Wheat: Selected Poems 1980-2015* (Picador, 2016) *On the Outskirts* (University of Queensland Press, 2017) and *Wound* (Arc Publications, 2018). His other recent books with Arc are *America (A Poem)* (2005) and *Comus: A Dialogic Mask* (2008). His volumes of stories include *In the Shade of the Shady Tree* (Ohio University Press, 2012), *Crow's Breath* (Transit Lounge, 2015) and *Old Growth* (Transit Lounge, 2017). His volumes of criticism include *Activist Poetics: Anarchy in the Avon Valley* (Liverpool University Press, 2010) and *Polysituatedness* (Manchester University Press, 2017).

He is a Fellow of Churchill College, Cambridge University, and Professor of Literature and Environment at Curtin University, but most relevantly he is an anarchist vegan pacifist of over thirty years. He believes poetry is one of the most effective activist modes of expression and resistance we have.

STEPHEN CHINNA is a Senior Honorary Research Fellow at the University of Western Australia. As well as teaching in English and Cultural Studies, his major teaching and research interests are in theatre and performance studies as well as creative writing for the stage. He has directed over thirty theatre productions at the university. In May 2001 he directed a production of *Smith Street (Between Heaven and Hell)* by John Kinsella and Tracy Ryan, as well as contributing material to the script. In February 2003, he directed and acted in a moved reading of John Kinsella's *The Wasps* at Trinity College, Cambridge in collaboration with the Marlowe Society.

TIM CRIBB is a Fellow of Churchill College, Cambridge, where he recently retired as Director of Studies in English and Tutor for Advanced Students. He was an undergraduate at Cambridge, a graduate teaching assistant at the University of Minnesota and a postgraduate at Oxford, where he pursued research on Dickens. Before returning to Cambridge, he was a lecturer at the University of Glasgow.

Throughout the '60s and '70s he acted in summer seasons at the Minack Theatre in Cornwall. During 1977-78 he was seconded as Visiting Senior Lecturer to the University of Ife (Nigeria) where he adapted and directed one of Yeats's plays for the University theatre company. He has directed a number of productions in Cambridge, including plays by Pablo Neruda, Bertolt Brecht, Wole Soyinka and John Kinsella's first play, *Crop Circles* (1998).

Among his other interests are Shakespeare and the Anglophone literature of the Caribbean, especially Wilson Harris and Derek Walcott. He is editor of *Imagined Commonwealths: Cambridge Essays on Commonwealth and International Literature in English* (Macmillan, 1999) and of *The Power of the Word / La Puissance du Verbe* (Rodopi, 2006) and author of *Bloomsbury and British Theatre: the Marlowe Story* (Salt, 2007). He is Senior Treasurer of Cambridge University Marlowe Society.

He is married, with one daughter, and lives in Cambridge.

CPSIA information can be obtained
at www.ICGtesting.com
Printed in the USA
BVHW030220020519
547187BV00001B/71/P

9 781911 469551